Birds of
MARYLAND

FIELD GUIDE & LOGBOOK

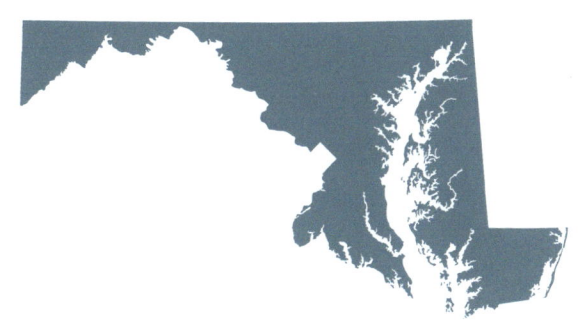

ALAN RINTOUL

TABLE OF CONTENTS

TABLE OF CONTENTS

TABLE OF CONTENTS

MEET THE AUTHOR

Alan Rintoul is a passionate birdwatcher and nature lover in his early 50s. For decades, he's wandered forests, wetlands, coastlines, and open fields with binoculars around his neck and a field guide in hand. What began as a peaceful hobby quickly grew into a lifelong passion—one that he shared deeply with his late wife, his closest companion on countless birdwatching journeys across the United States and Central America.

Together, they turned every trip into a chance to learn, observe, and appreciate the beauty of birds and the quiet magic of the natural world. After her passing, Alan found solace in returning to the wild places they once explored together. With every birdsong and fluttering wing, he feels her presence still walking beside him.

Today, Alan continues to travel across the country, searching for rare species, observing seasonal migrations, and learning something new with every outing. He believes birdwatching is more than a pastime—it's a way to slow down, reconnect with nature, and find moments of peace and wonder in the everyday world.

Through this guide, Alan hopes to share his love of birds with others. Whether you're just beginning your birdwatching journey or deep into your own lifelong adventure, he invites you to join him in discovering the joy, beauty, and meaning that birds can bring into our lives.

WELCOME TO BIRDWATCHING IN MARYLAND

Maryland sits where the Atlantic Ocean meets the nation's largest estuary and where ancient ridges rise in the west. Within a morning's drive you can stand on an Assateague dune scanning for pelicans, then finish the day listening for thrushes in an old-growth hemlock grove near the Youghiogheny River. Such tight-packed diversity makes the Free State one of the most rewarding birding arenas on the Atlantic Coast.

This guide is built to help you explore that richness. Inside you'll meet 60 Maryland birds—arranged into songbirds, raptors, and waterbirds—each profile offering crisp ID notes, natural-history highlights, and a fun fact to spark wonder on the trail.

More than a book, it's a companion. A logbook in the back lets you chronicle sightings, weather, and impressions so every warbler flit or eagle stoop becomes part of your personal birding story.

A Land of Sky and Song

Though barely 250 miles long, Maryland spans coastal plain, tidal marsh, Piedmont forest, and Appalachian highlands. Its position on the Atlantic Flyway funnels millions of migrants each spring and fall—snow geese cloud the Eastern Shore, while warblers pour through wooded ravines of the west.

Winter brings vast rafts of ducks and swans to the Chesapeake, especially the protected pools of Blackwater National Wildlife Refuge. In summer, salty marshes buzz with seaside sparrows and clapper rails, and osprey nests seem to crown every channel marker.

Maryland's state bird, the brilliant Baltimore Oriole, threads bright song through riparian sycamores—an emblem of the state's intertwined urban and wild landscapes.

From barrier-island beaches to moss-draped mountain hollows, the terrain is stitched together by rivers that carry both birds and birders toward new discoveries.

A Glimpse of What Awaits

Mountain & Highland Birds – In Garrett County's cool spruce and hemlock, listen for Black-throated Green and Canada Warblers, or spot Common Ravens soaring over rocky outcrops.

- **Raptors:** Conowingo Dam is legendary for winter concentrations of Bald Eagles; autumn hawk watches along South Mountain add broad-winged kettles and peregrine stoops.

- **Waterbirds & Wetland Species:** Tundra Swans, Canvasbacks, and Northern Pintails crowd Eastern Neck and Blackwater refuges from November through February.

- **Songbirds & Warblers:** Spring fallout along the Susquehanna River can deliver 30 warbler species in a morning, including globally-threatened Cerulean Warblers.

- **Maryland Specialties:** Look for Brown-headed Nuthatches squeaking in Eastern-Shore pines, Seaside Sparrows skulking in tidal cordgrass, and the secretive King Rail in brackish marshes.

Made for Learning, Built for Logging

Whether you're picking out your first field marks or polishing a 300-species state list, this guide offers clear information and a ready space for notes. Use the profiles to prepare, then jot impressions in the logbook—the smells of marsh mud, the color of dawn over Chesapeake water—so memory stays as vivid as plumage.

BEST PLACES TO BIRDWATCH IN MARYLAND

Though small in size, Maryland boasts remarkable bird diversity. From Atlantic barrier islands and tidal marshes to mountain gorges and river valleys, the state offers a stunning variety of birding opportunities across the seasons.

Whether you're after wintering waterfowl, marshland specialists, or springtime warbler waves, these top spots promise memorable sightings for birders of all levels.

Blackwater National Wildlife Refuge

Located on the lower Eastern Shore, Blackwater's vast tidal marshes attract tens of thousands of wintering waterfowl. It's also one of the best places in the East to spot Bald Eagles year-round.

Top Birds to Spot: Tundra Swan, Northern Pintail, Bald Eagle, Seaside Sparrow

Best Time to Visit: Mid-October to mid-March for waterfowl; spring for songbirds

Assateague Island National Seashore

This barrier island along the Atlantic Flyway offers beaches, dunes, and maritime forests. It's a hotspot for migratory shorebirds, sea-watching, and even winter rarities like Snowy Owls.

Top Birds to Spot: Piping Plover, Red Knot, Black Skimmer, Tricolored Heron

Best Time to Visit: Spring and fall migration; winter for sea birds

Patuxent Research Refuge

Tucked between Washington and Baltimore, this 13,000-acre refuge supports forest, meadow, and wetland birds. Established for research, it's also a great place to spot breeding songbirds.

Top Birds to Spot: Scarlet Tanager, Prothonotary Warbler, Osprey, Wood Duck

Best Time to Visit: April to June for breeders; September for migrants

Conowingo Dam

One of the best Bald Eagle viewing areas on the East Coast, Conowingo Dam draws hundreds each winter to fish the Susquehanna River's rich waters.

Top Birds to Spot: Bald Eagle, Black-crowned Night-Heron, Bonaparte's Gull, Peregrine Falcon

Best Time to Visit: November to January

Point Lookout State Park

Where the Potomac River meets the Chesapeake Bay, this narrow peninsula channels migratory birds and has recorded nearly 300 species.

Top Birds to Spot: Red-headed Woodpecker, Northern Gannet, Connecticut Warbler, Seaside Sparrow

Best Time to Visit: April–May and August–October

C&O Canal National Historical Park

Stretching 185 miles along the Potomac, the park includes bottomland forest, river edge, and canal-side trails—ideal for both breeders and wintering birds.

Top Birds to Spot: Prothonotary Warbler, Yellow-crowned Night-Heron, Tundra Swan, Rusty Blackbird

Best Time to Visit: April to June for breeding species; December to February for waterfowl

Eastern Neck National Wildlife Refuge

This island refuge in the Chester River hosts wintering swan flocks and nesting eagles, and features accessible trails through marsh and woodland.

Top Birds to Spot: Tundra Swan, Brown-headed Nuthatch, American Avocet, Yellow-throated Warbler

Best Time to Visit: Mid-November to February for swans; May for songbirds

Susquehanna State Park

Just south of Conowingo, this park's mature woods and bluffs are Maryland's best spot for Cerulean Warblers and a thoroughfare for migrating passerines.

Top Birds to Spot: Cerulean Warbler, Yellow-throated Vireo, Osprey, Common Loon

Best Time to Visit: Early May and early September

Hart-Miller Island State Park

Accessible only by boat, this dredge-spoil island in the Chesapeake Bay has logged over 300 species, making it a magnet for shorebirds and marsh sparrows.

Top Birds to Spot: American Avocet, Baird's Sandpiper, Gull-billed Tern, Nelson's Sparrow

Best Time to Visit: May to June and August to October

Swallow Falls State Park

Located in Maryland's western highlands, this park's ancient hemlock groves and cool mountain streams support high-elevation species rarely seen elsewhere in the state.

Top Birds to Spot: Canada Warbler, Black-throated Green Warbler, Dark-eyed Junco, Pileated Woodpecker

Best Time to Visit: Late May to August

These ten destinations are just the beginning. From forested piedmonts to windswept coasts, Maryland's public lands and diverse habitats offer rewarding birding for every season—and every birder.

BIRDWATCHING ETHICS & ETIQUETTE

Birdwatching is more than just observing wildlife—it's about forming a respectful relationship with nature. As birders, we have a responsibility to minimize our impact, protect habitats, and ensure that future generations can experience the same joy of discovering birds in the wild.

Whether you're deep in the wetlands or walking a suburban trail, the way you conduct yourself matters. Following basic birdwatching ethics not only benefits the birds—it also creates a more meaningful and rewarding experience for you and those around you.

Keep a Safe and Respectful Distance

Getting too close to a bird—especially during nesting season—can cause stress or even force it to abandon its nest. Always observe birds from a distance using binoculars or a zoom lens. If a bird changes its behavior because of your presence, you're likely too close.

Stay on Trails and Boardwalks

Wandering off-path may damage fragile habitats and disturb ground-nesting species. Many protected areas were designed with bird safety in mind. By sticking to designated walkways, you help preserve these environments and reduce your impact.

Avoid Disturbing Nests and Roosts

Nests and roosting areas are critical for breeding and resting. Avoid lingering near them, never touch or photograph nests up close, and resist the temptation to clear vegetation for a better view. Birds need privacy, especially during vulnerable stages.

Limit the Use of Bird Calls and Playback

While bird calls played from apps or devices can be helpful in identification, overusing them can disrupt a bird's natural behavior—drawing it out unnecessarily or causing stress. Use playback sparingly and only in situations where it's allowed and ethical.

Respect Fellow Birders and Wildlife Enthusiasts

Keep noise levels low, especially in quiet areas. Share spotting opportunities with others when possible, and be courteous when using shared spaces like observation decks or narrow trails. Everyone is there to enjoy nature—your presence should enhance, not hinder, the experience.

Leave No Trace

Pack out everything you bring in, including snacks, field notes, and wrappers. Litter not only ruins the natural setting but also poses a danger to wildlife. A clean environment is safer for birds and more enjoyable for birders.

Report Unusual Sightings Responsibly

If you spot a rare bird, be cautious when sharing the location publicly. Large crowds can quickly descend on sensitive habitats and disturb the birds. Consider reporting to local birding groups or eBird with habitat sensitivity in mind.

Support Conservation Efforts

Whenever possible, donate to or volunteer with organizations that protect birds and their habitats. Your time and resources can help preserve migration routes, nesting grounds, and public access to birding spaces.

Birdwatching is built on patience, quiet observation, and appreciation. By following these simple practices, you become a steward of the wild places and winged creatures that bring so much beauty into our lives.

Let the birds guide you—not just to sightings, but to a deeper respect for the world we share.

HOW TO USE THIS BOOK

This guide was designed to be both beautiful and practical, whether you're flipping through it at home, reviewing your sightings over coffee, or carrying it with you on the trail. With a focus on 60 carefully selected bird species, it serves as both a field guide for learning and a logbook for recording your birdwatching experiences.

Each bird is presented in a clean, easy-to-read format that gives you quick access to essential identification details and fascinating facts. But beyond names and numbers, this book encourages a deeper connection with the birds you encounter—inviting you to observe, reflect, and document what you discover along the way.

Whether you're learning your first warblers or keeping track of your favorite raptors, this guide is made to support your journey one page, one feathered friend at a time.

Here's what you'll find in every bird profile:

1. Bird Name & Pronunciation

At the top of each page, you'll find the common name of the bird, along with a phonetic pronunciation to help you say it correctly in the field.

2. Full-Color Image

A high-quality photo gives you a clear visual reference to help with identification.

3. Description Paragraph

This section gives a quick but vivid overview of the bird's personality, behavior, and habitat. It often includes interesting traits, feeding habits, nesting behavior, and how they interact with humans or other animals.

4. Fact Box

Below the main paragraph, you'll find a quick-reference list with key details:
- **Scientific Name**
- **Habitat**
- **Diet**
- **Size / Weight**
- **Lifespan**
- **Nesting Habits**
- **Eggs**
- **Predators**

These facts are helpful for both learning and field identification.

5. Fun Fact: "Did You Know..."

Each bird entry ends with a quirky or fascinating tidbit—a unique behavior, adaptation, or lesser-known fact to deepen your appreciation for the species.

Tips for Using This Book in the Field

- Flip to the profile that matches the bird you've spotted for quick confirmation and ID.
- Use the habitat and behavior notes to narrow down what bird you're seeing.
- Compare your sightings with the images and descriptions to build confidence in your identification.
- Carry a pencil or pen and make quick notes in the logbook section at the back of the book to record date, location, and personal observations.

A separate "How to Use the Birdwatching Log" page is included later in the book, just before the log section begins. That page will help you understand how to use the log pages effectively, whether you're keeping a casual record or building a serious bird list over time.

Wherever your birdwatching journey takes you—city park, coastal marsh, forest trail, or backyard feeder—this book is here to guide you, educate you, and help you create lasting memories of the birds you meet.

BACKYARD
& SONGBIRDS

Baltimore Oriole is a glowing beacon of color in Maryland's leafy neighborhoods, forest edges, and streamside groves. Males wear blazing orange and deep black, while females show softer orange-yellow hues with grayish tones. Their hanging, woven nests are intricate sacs suspended high in trees, built with grass, hair, and plant fiber. These orioles arrive in late April, filling the air with rich whistles that drift through the treetops. Often seen in pairs, they forage for insects and sip nectar from blooms or feeders. Backyard birders attract them with orange halves or grape jelly—favorites during migration and nesting. By late summer, family groups visit fruiting trees before heading south. They molt into fresh plumage just before departing, leaving in peak brightness. Orioles favor tall shade trees and quiet woodlands for breeding, avoiding heavily urbanized areas.

- **Scientific Name:** Icterus galbula
- **Habitat:** Forest edges, tall trees, suburban yards
- **Diet:** Insects, fruit, nectar, caterpillars
- **Size / Weight:** 7–8¾ in / around 1.1 oz
- **Lifespan:** Up to 11 years wild
- **Nesting Habits:** Pouch-like nest, hung 20–40 ft high
- **Eggs:** 3–7 pale blue, finely scrawled
- **Predators:** Crows, squirrels, jays, climbing snakes

DID YOU KNOW...

Female orioles may stitch over 10,000 fibers into one nest, crafting a hanging cradle without reusing last year's work.

Flashing crimson against snow or spring buds, the Northern Cardinal is Maryland's most familiar year-round songbird. Males blaze red with a black face mask, while females glow tan with peachy highlights. Both sexes sing cheer-cheer-cheer songs from trees and hedgerows, brightening early mornings. Cardinals are fiercely territorial, sometimes attacking their reflections in windows. Pairs often mate for life and raise multiple broods in well-hidden shrub nests. Their thick orange bills crack seeds with ease, making feeders ideal gathering spots. They don't migrate and stay active even in winter, adding color to snowy backyards. Their signature red comes from carotenoid-rich berries and seeds. Friendly and bold, cardinals thrive in suburban landscapes across the state.

- **Scientific Name:** Cardinalis cardinalis
- **Habitat:** Thickets, forest edges, suburban gardens, brushy fields
- **Diet:** Seeds, berries, insects
- **Size / Weight:** 8–9 in / 1.5–1.8 oz
- **Lifespan:** Up to 15 years; most live 3–5 years
- **Nesting Habits:** Open cup, 3–10 ft high in dense shrubs or vines
- **Eggs:** 2–5 whitish with brown speckles; 11–13 day incubation
- **Predators:** Hawks, snakes, domestic cats

DID YOU KNOW...

Because cardinals add red pigment from food, captive birds on low-carotenoid diets can tfade to pale brown—proof that you truly are what you eat!

3- AMERICAN ROBIN *(uh-meh-rih-kuhn rah-bin)*

The American Robin is a cheerful and adaptable songbird found throughout Maryland's woodlands, parks, farms, and backyards. With its orange breast, gray upperparts, and yellow bill, it's one of the most recognizable birds in the state. Robins are early signs of spring, often beginning their mud-lined nests in late winter. Females handle all nest building and incubation, while males stand guard and sing clear, fluty phrases from high perches. They forage for worms and insects on lawns, tilting their heads to spot movement, and later switch to berries such as holly, dogwood, and juniper in fall and winter. Robins may raise two or three broods per season, using trees, ledges, and even porch lights as nest sites. Though seen alone in summer, they flock in colder months and roam in search of food. Friendly and ever-present, they are a comforting emblem of seasonal change across the state.

- **Scientific Name:** Turdus migratorius
- **Habitat:** Lawns, forests, parks, farmland
- **Diet:** Earthworms, insects, berries
- **Size / Weight:** 9–11 in / 2.5–3 oz
- **Lifespan:** Typically 2 years; up to 14 recorded
- **Nesting Habits:** Mud-lined cup on branches or structures
- **Eggs:** 3–4 blue eggs; 12–14 day incubation
- **Predators:** Hawks, snakes, squirrels, cats

DID YOU KNOW...

Robins locate worms mostly by sight, not sound, using head tilts to focus each eye. Their vivid blue eggs are so iconic they inspired a classic paint color, and their song is often one of the first heard at dawn in spring.

The Carolina Wren is a bold, year-round Maryland resident known for its loud teakettle-teakettle song and spunky personality. Its rich chestnut back, buff belly, and crisp white eyebrow stripe make it easy to recognize when it ventures from dense cover. Pairs bond for life and remain on territory together, nesting in cavities and quirky places like boots, mailboxes, or flowerpots. Their domed nests are built from leaves, bark, feathers, and string, often hidden close to human activity. These wrens forage by hopping low through brush and leaf litter in search of insects, spiders, and suet in winter. They raise multiple broods and rely on dense shelter during snow and ice. While shy in presence, they're loud in song and heard far more than seen. Their cheerful voice rings through forests, yards, and porches, announcing their place in Maryland's backyards all year long.

- **Scientific Name:** Thryothorus ludovicianus
- **Habitat:** Brush, forests, gardens, porches, woodpiles
- **Diet:** Insects, spiders, berries, suet
- **Size / Weight:** 5.5 in / 0.6–0.8 oz
- **Lifespan:** Average 2 years; up to 6–7
- **Nesting Habits:** Domed nest in cavities or odd places
- **Eggs:** 4–6 white with brown spots; 12–16 day incubation
- **Predators:** Cats, raccoons, jays, snakes

DID YOU KNOW...

Carolina Wrens sing through all seasons, even in snow. Their voice is so powerful for their size that many birders hear them long before they're seen, especially around backyard sheds and tangled vines.

The Song Sparrow is one of Maryland's most widespread and familiar sparrows, with brown streaks, a dark chest spot, and a sweet, buzzy voice. Males sing from low branches, shrubs, or fences, especially in early spring, and may repeat tunes all day to mark territory and attract mates. Their songs vary across regions, giving rise to local "dialects." These birds nest low in grasses, shrubs, or brush piles, weaving well-hidden cup nests lined with grass and fur. Females do most of the building and incubating, while males guard and sing nearby. They raise multiple broods, often in the same general area. Song Sparrows forage for insects in summer and seeds in colder months, frequently seen scratching beneath feeders. Their shy yet persistent nature and adaptability to both wild and suburban habitats make them one of the most reliable backyard birds across the state.

- **Scientific Name:** Melospiza melodia
- **Habitat:** Fields, marshes, thickets, suburbs
- **Diet:** Seeds, insects, spiders
- **Size / Weight:** 5–6.5 in / 0.5–1.4 oz
- **Lifespan:** 2–3 years average; up to 11
- **Nesting Habits:** Low cup nest in grass or brush
- **Eggs:** 3–5 bluish-green with spots; 12–14 day incubation
- **Predators:** Hawks, cats, snakes, crows

DID YOU KNOW...

Each male Song Sparrow sings a unique mix of melodies. They learn songs from nearby adults, not their parents, leading to regional accents and variations across Maryland's habitats.

Gray Catbird is a smooth, slate-colored mimic with a black cap, rusty undertail, and an endlessly inventive voice. Named for its cat-like "mew" call, it's best known for weaving together songs borrowed from other birds, frogs, and even machines into long, improvisational performances. Catbirds prefer dense vegetation—thickets, shrubs, and tangles near water or gardens—where they sing loudly from hidden perches. They arrive in Maryland by late spring and build bulky, twiggy cup nests low in shrubs or vines. Females do most of the construction, while males sing and defend the area. Their diet includes insects, fruit, and berries, with pokeweed and elderberry favorites in late summer. Though often secretive, they grow bold around fruiting plants and birdbaths. Their presence is easiest to confirm by sound, making them a favorite among attentive backyard birders.

- **Scientific Name:** Dumetella carolinensis
- **Habitat:** Shrubby edges, thickets, hedgerows, suburban gardens
- **Diet:** Insects, berries, fruit
- **Size / Weight:** 8–9.5 in / 0.8–1.2 oz
- **Lifespan:** 2.5 years average; up to 10
- **Nesting Habits:** Open cup in shrubs or vines
- **Eggs:** 3–5 turquoise eggs; 12–15 day incubation
- **Predators:** Jays, snakes, cats, raccoons

DID YOU KNOW...

Gray Catbirds mimic over 100 different sounds, often without repeating. Males sing from deep within shrubs, and their secretive behavior keeps them well-hidden even in busy backyards.

7- EASTERN BLUEBIRD *(ee-stern bloo-berd)*

Eastern Bluebird is a gentle, vibrant thrush with deep sky-blue wings and a rusty orange chest, glowing like a jewel against fields and fencerows. Males are more brightly colored, but females share the same soft tones. They prefer open spaces with scattered trees and nest in cavities—natural or manmade—making nest boxes vital for their success. Bluebirds pair up early in spring and raise up to three broods, with males offering nesting sites and feeding mates. They perch patiently before dropping to the ground to snag insects or snatch caterpillars midair. In cooler months, they form small flocks and switch to berries, including dogwood and juniper. Bluebirds once declined due to competition for nest cavities, but conservation efforts have reversed that trend. Their quiet, whistled calls and peaceful demeanor make them a favorite of backyard birders throughout Maryland's countryside.

- **Scientific Name:** Sialia sialis
- **Habitat:** Open fields, orchards, pastures, forest edges
- **Diet:** Insects, spiders, berries
- **Size / Weight:** 6.5–7.5 in / 1.0–1.1 oz
- **Lifespan:** 6–10 years; many die earlier
- **Nesting Habits:** Cavities or nest boxes, 3–20 ft high
- **Eggs:** 4–6 pale blue eggs; 13–16 day incubation
- **Predators:** Snakes, raccoons, cats, starlings

DID YOU KNOW...

Bluebird populations rebounded thanks to nest box trails. Providing clean, monitored boxes can support generations of local birds in your area.

8- TUFTED TITMOUSE *(tuhf-tid tit-mows)*

The Tufted Titmouse is a compact gray songbird with a big personality, marked by its perky crest, black forehead, and peachy flanks. Common across Maryland woodlands and backyards, it travels in small flocks with chickadees and nuthatches, chattering in high whistles—peter-peter-peter. These birds are agile and bold, hanging upside down to inspect leaves and bark for insects or grabbing seeds from feeders. They nest in natural cavities or old woodpecker holes, often lining their nests with hair, feathers, or fur. Pairs bond long-term and may remain together all year. Titmice store food in bark or crevices to retrieve later and quickly adapt to winter feeders. Their sharp curiosity and bright presence make them a constant delight in any yard, forest edge, or neighborhood park.

- **Scientific Name:** Baeolophus bicolor
- **Habitat:** Deciduous woods, suburbs, parks, orchards
- **Diet:** Insects, seeds, berries, nuts
- **Size / Weight:** 5.5–6.3 in / 0.6–0.9 oz
- **Lifespan:** Typically 2.1 years; some reach 10
- **Nesting Habits:** Cavities lined with animal fur or hair
- **Eggs:** 5–7 speckled white eggs; 12–14 day incubation
- **Predators:** Hawks, owls, cats, snakes

DID YOU KNOW...

Tufted Titmice sometimes pluck hair from live animals for nest lining—dogs, raccoons, even people aren't off-limits!

Bold, brilliant, and brimming with personality, the Blue Jay is a striking backyard visitor with a bright blue back, white face, and black necklace. It mimics hawk calls, rattles, and whistles and may alert or confuse other birds with its sounds. Found statewide in forests and neighborhoods, jays are clever foragers that cache acorns and peanuts for later. They travel in family groups and can be aggressive at feeders but also help plant trees by burying seeds they forget. Blue Jays build large, open-cup nests in trees and defend them fiercely. They eat a mix of insects, nuts, seeds, and the occasional bird egg. Their social nature, intelligence, and vivid colors make them one of Maryland's most visible and vocal songbirds, easily recognized by their flight calls and flashes of electric blue.

- **Scientific Name:** Cyanocitta cristata
- **Habitat:** Deciduous woods, suburbs, groves
- **Diet:** Nuts, seeds, insects, berries
- **Size / Weight:** 9–12 in / 2.5–3.5 oz
- **Lifespan:** 6–7 years average; some reach 17+
- **Nesting Habits:** Tree branches, 10–25 ft high
- **Eggs:** 3–6 light blue or olive eggs; 16–18 day incubation
- **Predators:** Hawks, owls, snakes, cats

DID YOU KNOW...

Blue Jays can imitate Red-shouldered Hawks and may use this mimicry to test safety or scare other birds away from food.

The Chipping Sparrow is a trim, energetic bird with a rusty cap, clear gray breast, and a black line through the eye. These sparrows are found throughout Maryland in spring and summer, hopping through grassy lawns, open woods, or along woodland edges. They forage on the ground for seeds and insects, often appearing tame around people. Their song is a steady mechanical trill, usually delivered from a treetop or fencepost. Chipping Sparrows nest low in conifers or shrubs, weaving fine grasses into neat, open cups. They raise one or two broods, and parents may feed fledglings for weeks after they leave the nest. In fall, they gather into flocks and migrate south, returning in early spring. Light and fast, they're a frequent visitor to feeders and garden edges during breeding season.

- **Scientific Name:** Spizella passerina
- **Habitat:** Open woods, yards, clearings, parks
- **Diet:** Seeds, insects, grasshoppers
- **Size / Weight:** 4.5–5.5 in / 0.4–0.6 oz
- **Lifespan:** Up to 9 years; most live 2–3
- **Nesting Habits:** Shrubs or evergreens, 3–10 ft high
- **Eggs:** 3–4 pale blue eggs; 10–12 day incubation
- **Predators:** Jays, snakes, cats, raccoons

DID YOU KNOW...

Chipping Sparrows get their name from their sharp, high "chip" call. Males return to the same breeding territory each year with amazing precision.

11- DOWNY WOODPECKER *(dow-nee)*

The Downy Woodpecker is Maryland's smallest woodpecker, with bold black-and-white plumage and a crisp white back. Males have a small red patch on the back of the head, while females are black-capped. These friendly woodpeckers are common in forests, parks, and suburban yards year-round, often found flitting among tree trunks or visiting suet feeders. They drum on trees and metal poles to signal territory and tap lightly for insects hiding under bark. Downies nest in tree cavities excavated by both sexes and may reuse favorite trees for several seasons. They forage using short hops and cling sideways on thin stems, unlike larger woodpeckers. Their soft pik call and whinnying trill are often heard before the bird is seen. Easily approachable and active even in winter, the Downy Woodpecker is a favorite among backyard birders of all ages.

- **Scientific Name:** Dryobates pubescens
- **Habitat:** Woodlands, yards, orchards, parks
- **Diet:** Insects, sap, seeds, suet
- **Size / Weight:** 5.5–6.7 in / 0.7–1.0 oz
- **Lifespan:** Up to 11 years; average 2–3
- **Nesting Habits:** Tree cavities, often in dead limbs
- **Eggs:** 3–6 white eggs; 12-day incubation
- **Predators:** Hawks, snakes, squirrels, cats

DID YOU KNOW...

Downy Woodpeckers often forage with chickadees and titmice. They're so light they can feed from thin weed stems most woodpeckers ignore.

Despite its name, the Red-bellied Woodpecker is best known for its vivid red crown and nape, not its faintly blushed belly. Common across Maryland's woodlands and neighborhoods, this medium-sized woodpecker clings to trunks and large branches, often calling with a rolling churr. Its black-and-white barred back makes it easy to distinguish from others. Males and females excavate cavity nests in dead trees or limbs, sometimes returning to the same site each year. They eat beetles, caterpillars, nuts, fruit, and suet, and frequently visit feeders. Red-bellied Woodpeckers cache food in bark crevices, storing it for leaner months. Agile and acrobatic, they hitch up trees and even feed upside down. Their loud calls and striking markings make them easy to spot in any season, whether deep in the woods or near backyard feeders.

- **Scientific Name:** Melanerpes carolinus
- **Habitat:** Woodlands, parks, yards, river bottoms
- **Diet:** Insects, nuts, fruit, suet
- **Size / Weight:** 9–10.5 in / 2.0–3.2 oz
- **Lifespan:** 4–12 years in the wild
- **Nesting Habits:** Tree cavities 5–70 ft above ground
- **Eggs:** 3–5 white eggs; 12-day incubation
- **Predators:** Hawks, snakes, squirrels, cats

DID YOU KNOW...

The red "belly" is usually hidden from view. Their rolling, laughing calls are among the most distinctive sounds in Maryland forests.

The House Finch is a friendly, social songbird with streaky brown plumage and, in males, a bright red crown, throat, and chest. Found in neighborhoods, farms, and city centers across Maryland, they nest on ledges, vents, hanging planters, and other built structures. Originally a western species, House Finches spread rapidly east after being introduced in New York in the 1940s. They forage in flocks and sing cheerful, warbling songs from rooftops, trees, and telephone wires. Seeds and buds form the bulk of their diet, but they also eat fruits and will flock to feeders stocked with sunflower. Pairs may raise several broods per year, and young finches remain in family groups after fledging. Though susceptible to eye disease at feeders, they remain one of the state's most visible backyard residents, often heard before seen.

- **Scientific Name:** Haemorhous mexicanus
- **Habitat:** Towns, suburbs, farms, open woods
- **Diet:** Seeds, buds, berries
- **Size / Weight:** 5–6 in / 0.6–0.9 oz
- **Lifespan:** Typically 3–6 years; max around 11
- **Nesting Habits:** Structures, ledges, planters, tree cavities
- **Eggs:** 2–6 pale blue eggs; 12–14 day incubation
- **Predators:** Cats, jays, hawks, snakes

DID YOU KNOW...

The red in male House Finches comes from pigments in their food. More colorful males tend to be more attractive to females.

The White-throated Sparrow is a plump, ground-foraging sparrow with bold facial stripes and a bright white throat bordered by a dark edge. It winters in Maryland in large numbers and breeds far to the north in Canadian forests. These sparrows scratch in leaf litter under shrubs and thickets, searching for seeds, berries, and insects. Males sing a mournful oh-sweet-Canada whistle from low branches or brush. Two color morphs—white-striped and tan-striped—differ in behavior, with white-stripes more aggressive and vocal. Both forms can be seen at backyard feeders, especially near hedges and brush piles. In spring, they migrate north in flocks, often heard before seen. Their soft colors, distinctive markings, and rich song make them a winter favorite across the state's wooded neighborhoods and parks.

- **Scientific Name:** Zonotrichia albicollis
- **Habitat:** Wooded edges, hedgerows, suburbs
- **Diet:** Seeds, berries, insects
- **Size / Weight:** 6–7.5 in / 0.8–1.1 oz
- **Lifespan:** 9 years maximum; average 2–3
- **Nesting Habits:** Northern breeder, nests on forest floor
- **Eggs:** 3–5 greenish-blue eggs; 11–14 day incubation
- **Predators:** Cats, hawks, jays, snakes

DID YOU KNOW...

White-throated Sparrows hybridize by personality—white- and tan-striped birds usually pair with the opposite type for balance.

15- AMERICAN GOLDFINCH *(gold-finch)*

The American Goldfinch is a bright, bouncy finch known for its cheerful, roller-coaster flight and bubbly calls. Males in summer shine lemon-yellow with black wings and caps, while females and winter birds are paler olive with muted markings. Common across Maryland year-round, goldfinches favor weedy fields, gardens, and feeders stocked with nyjer or sunflower. They're late nesters, waiting until July or August when thistle and milkweed seeds are abundant. Nests are tightly woven cups built in shrubs or saplings, often hidden in field edges. Both parents feed the young, relying heavily on seeds rather than insects. Goldfinches travel in loose flocks through all seasons and chatter constantly as they feed. Their flight is undulating and accompanied by a per-chick-o-ree call that makes them easy to recognize even in motion.

- **Scientific Name:** Spinus tristis
- **Habitat:** Meadows, gardens, fields, roadsides
- **Diet:** Seeds, buds, some insects
- **Size / Weight:** 4.3–5.1 in / 0.4–0.7 oz
- **Lifespan:** Typically 3–6 years; up to 11
- **Nesting Habits:** Shrubs or trees in open areas
- **Eggs:** 4–6 pale blue eggs; 12–14 day incubation
- **Predators:** Hawks, snakes, squirrels, cats

DID YOU KNOW...

American Goldfinches are the latest nesters of all Maryland songbirds. Their entire nesting season is timed to coincide with the peak of native seed production, especially thistles and sunflowers, which they depend on for feeding young.

The House Wren is a small, energetic brown bird with a bubbly personality and a voice that far outsizes its frame. Found in backyards and thickets across Maryland from spring to fall, it sings a fast, cheerful trill from fenceposts, shrubs, or rooflines. Males arrive first and stuff multiple cavities with twigs to attract mates, who choose one to complete for nesting. They readily use nest boxes, flowerpots, and even old boots. Wrens are fierce defenders of territory and will remove eggs from other birds' nests. They feed on spiders, beetles, and caterpillars, darting through low brush with a flicking tail. After raising 1–2 broods, most migrate south by October. Their adaptability and lively songs make them a welcome visitor in gardens and parks.

- **Scientific Name:** Troglodytes aedon
- **Habitat:** Suburbs, parks, woodland edges, yards
- **Diet:** Insects, spiders, beetles
- **Size / Weight:** 4.3–5.1 in / 0.3–0.4 oz
- **Lifespan:** 2–5 years; up to 9
- **Nesting Habits:** Cavities or nest boxes, filled with twigs
- **Eggs:** 5–8 pinkish eggs; 12–15 day incubation
- **Predators:** Cats, snakes, raccoons, jays

DID YOU KNOW...

House Wrens have one of the largest breeding ranges of any songbird in the Americas and are known for their ruthless nest competition—even destroying the eggs of chickadees or bluebirds.

17- CAROLINA CHICKADEE *(chik-uh-dee)*

Tiny, curious, and charmingly bold, the Carolina Chickadee sports a black cap and bib, white cheeks, and soft gray body. Found year-round throughout Maryland's woodlands and neighborhoods, it flits through trees in small flocks, issuing cheerful chick-a-dee-dee calls. They excavate or repurpose cavities in dead trees, lining nests with moss, bark, and hair. Chickadees cache food in bark and crevices and can remember these spots for weeks. Pairs bond early and may remain together for multiple seasons. They feed on insects, seeds, and suet, and are among the first to visit feeders each morning. Though similar to Black-capped Chickadees, Carolina Chickadees are smaller and more common in the southern half of the state. Friendly, vocal, and adaptable, they bring joy to backyard birders even in winter.

- **Scientific Name:** Poecile carolinensis
- **Habitat:** Forests, neighborhoods, parks, groves
- **Diet:** Insects, seeds, berries, suet
- **Size / Weight:** 4–5 in / 0.3–0.4 oz
- **Lifespan:** Typically 2–4 years; up to 10
- **Nesting Habits:** Cavities, often in dead wood or stumps
- **Eggs:** 5–8 white eggs; 12–15 day incubation
- **Predators:** Hawks, owls, snakes, cats

DID YOU KNOW...

Chickadees adjust their calls based on threat level. More dee notes in chick-a-dee-dee mean greater danger, alerting others in the flock.

The Ruby-throated Hummingbird is Maryland's only breeding hummingbird, dazzling observers with its shimmering green back and the male's iridescent red throat. Just over three inches long, it hovers with rapid wingbeats and feeds on nectar and insects. These hummingbirds arrive in April and leave by early fall, migrating across the Gulf of Mexico to wintering grounds in Central America. They're fiercely territorial, defending flower patches and feeders with swift aerial dives and buzzing chases. Females build delicate, camouflaged nests of plant fibers and spider silk on tree limbs. Though small, they have powerful memory and return to the same gardens year after year. They favor tubular flowers like trumpet vine and bee balm and readily use backyard sugar-water feeders.

- **Scientific Name:** Archilochus colubris
- **Habitat:** Gardens, woods, meadows, forest edges
- **Diet:** Nectar, insects, spiders
- **Size / Weight:** 3–3.5 in / 0.1–0.2 oz
- **Lifespan:** Typically 3–5 years; up to 9
- **Nesting Habits:** Tiny cups on branches 5–20 ft high
- **Eggs:** 2 white eggs; 12–14 day incubation
- **Predators:** Praying mantises, jays, snakes, cats

DID YOU KNOW...

Ruby-throated Hummingbirds beat their wings up to 80 times per second. Their hearts can race over 1,200 beats per minute while feeding.

Common Yellowthroat is a small, quick warbler of marshes and thickets, with males easily recognized by their bright yellow throats and bold black mask. Females are plainer but share the yellow wash. Their witchity-witchity-witchity song rings from cattails, brambles, and wet meadows across Maryland in spring and summer. They nest low in dense vegetation, weaving grass and reeds into hidden cups. Pairs raise one to two broods, and both adults stay close to the nest, carrying insects to hungry chicks. Yellowthroats forage by darting through underbrush in short hops, chasing down spiders, beetles, and caterpillars. They migrate at night, departing by fall for the southeastern U.S. and Central America. Despite their bold songs, they're often tricky to spot in thick cover.

- **Scientific Name:** Geothlypis trichas
- **Habitat:** Marshes, thickets, wet meadows, forest edges
- **Diet:** Insects, spiders, caterpillars
- **Size / Weight:** 4.3–5.1 in / 0.3–0.4 oz
- **Lifespan:** Up to 11 years; most live 2–3
- **Nesting Habits:** Ground-level cups in dense growth
- **Eggs:** 3–5 white eggs with spots; 12-day incubation
- **Predators:** Snakes, raccoons, crows, cats

DID YOU KNOW...

Though shy, male yellowthroats sing boldly from cover. Their black mask has earned them the nickname "bandit warbler" among birders.

The Eastern Towhee is a striking ground-dweller often found rustling through leaf litter beneath shrubs or forest edges. Males are bold black above with warm rufous flanks and white bellies; females are similar but rich brown instead of black. Their call—drink-your-tea!—rings out from thickets and hedgerows across Maryland in spring and summer. Towhees scratch with a double-hop motion to uncover insects, seeds, and berries hidden in the leaf litter. Nests are built low, often directly on the ground, and females incubate while males stand guard nearby. These birds prefer dense, tangled cover where they can remain hidden yet vocal. While they may visit brushy backyard edges, they're most easily spotted in wild or overgrown spaces. Despite their large size and bold colors, they often go unnoticed by casual observers unless they sing.

- **Scientific Name:** Pipilo erythrophthalmus
- **Habitat:** Brushy fields, forest edges, hedgerows
- **Diet:** Insects, seeds, berries
- **Size / Weight:** 7–8.5 in / 1.1–1.8 oz
- **Lifespan:** Typically 3–5 years; up to 9
- **Nesting Habits:** Low shrubs or on ground in cover
- **Eggs:** 3–5 spotted eggs; 12–13 day incubation
- **Predators:** Snakes, raccoons, jays, cats

DID YOU KNOW...

Eastern Towhees forage by hopping and scratching backward with both feet, a signature method that sends dry leaves flying and often reveals their hidden presence.

21- WOOD THRUSH *(wood thruhsh)*

The Wood Thrush is a secretive forest songbird with a cinnamon back, bold white chest, and dramatic black spots. Found in shady, mature woods across Maryland, it sings one of the most beautiful bird songs in North America—a flute-like ee-oh-lay echoing through early morning fog. Males use internal voice structures to sing in two harmonies at once. Wood Thrushes forage quietly on the forest floor for insects, spiders, and fallen berries. Their cup nests are built in shrubs or saplings, often hidden among dense undergrowth. They breed in late spring and summer, raising one or two broods. These birds are sensitive to habitat loss and fragmentation, declining in numbers despite their iconic song. Most migrate to Central America by mid-fall, returning the following spring to the same woods. Their haunting melodies remain a treasured sound in Maryland's protected forests.

- **Scientific Name:** Hylocichla mustelina
- **Habitat:** Deciduous forests, shady groves, riparian woods
- **Diet:** Insects, snails, berries
- **Size / Weight:** 7.5–8.5 in / 1.5–2.0 oz
- **Lifespan:** Typically 3–5 years; up to 8
- **Nesting Habits:** Cups in shrubs or small trees
- **Eggs:** 3–4 blue eggs; 12–13 day incubation
- **Predators:** Snakes, raccoons, jays, cowbirds

DID YOU KNOW...

Wood Thrushes can sing two notes at once thanks to a divided syrinx, producing rich, echoing phrases that many consider the finest of any North American bird.

Tiny, squeaky, and endlessly active, the Brown-headed Nuthatch is a specialty of pine forests and one of the few birds in Maryland restricted to the Eastern Shore. It's easily recognized by its warm brown cap, buffy underparts, and habit of creeping headfirst down pine trunks. Its call sounds like a rubber ducky squeak—sharp and high-pitched. These nuthatches forage for insects and pine seeds, using their bills to pry under bark. They nest in tree cavities and will readily use nest boxes placed in pine groves. Brown-headed Nuthatches are social and may form family groups, with young from previous years helping raise new chicks. They store food for winter and stay active year-round. Conservation of longleaf and loblolly pine habitats is crucial to maintaining their small state population.

- **Scientific Name:** Sitta pusilla
- **Habitat:** Coastal pine forests, groves, plantations
- **Diet:** Insects, spiders, pine seeds
- **Size / Weight:** 3.9–4.3 in / 0.3–0.4 oz
- **Lifespan:** Up to 7 years in the wild
- **Nesting Habits:** Tree cavities or nest boxes in pines
- **Eggs:** 4–6 white eggs; 14-day incubation
- **Predators:** Snakes, squirrels, woodpeckers, jays

DID YOU KNOW...

Brown-headed Nuthatches are one of few U.S. birds to show cooperative breeding—helpers assist parents in feeding nestlings and defending cavities.

23- SCARLET TANAGER *(skar-lit tan-uh-jer)*

The Scarlet Tanager is a dazzling summer visitor cloaked in forest shadows, with males in brilliant red plumage and black wings. Females wear greenish-yellow with darker wings, blending more easily into the treetops. These birds breed in mature deciduous forests across western and central Maryland and stay high in the canopy, where they sing a burry, robin-like tune. Tanagers are slow-moving and deliberate, gleaning insects from leaves and branches. Their nests are shallow cups placed far above the ground, hidden from view. They are among the first songbirds to migrate south in early fall, disappearing to the Andes by October. Their bold color and reclusive nature make them a top prize for spring birdwatchers, best seen where large forest tracts remain undisturbed.

- **Scientific Name:** Piranga olivacea
- **Habitat:** Mature deciduous forests, wooded hillsides
- **Diet:** Insects, berries, fruit
- **Size / Weight:** 6.5–7.5 in / 0.9–1.3 oz
- **Lifespan:** 5–6 years typical; up to 10
- **Nesting Habits:** Tree branches 20–50 ft above ground
- **Eggs:** 3–5 pale blue-green eggs; 13–14 day incubation
- **Predators:** Hawks, crows, squirrels, snakes

DID YOU KNOW...

Scarlet Tanagers molt their red feathers after breeding, becoming olive-yellow like females—a clever disguise for their long tropical migration.

Glowing yellow with blue-gray wings and a bold black eye, the Prothonotary Warbler is a radiant inhabitant of Maryland's swampy woods and bottomland forests. Unlike most warblers, it nests in tree cavities, usually in standing water near rivers or swamps. Males sing a loud, ringing tweet-tweet-tweet from willows and bald cypress, often near water's edge. Pairs line their cavities with moss, bark, and fine grass, sometimes nesting in boxes if placed properly near suitable habitat. They feed on caterpillars, beetles, and aquatic insects, and migrate to Central America in fall. Though scarce, they breed in reliable locations like Patuxent River and southern tidewater zones. Their golden glow among wetland shadows makes them one of the most sought-after warblers on Maryland's coastal plain.

- **Scientific Name:** Protonotaria citrea
- **Habitat:** Swamps, riversides, wooded wetlands
- **Diet:** Insects, spiders, snails
- **Size / Weight:** 5.1–5.5 in / 0.4–0.5 oz
- **Lifespan:** Typically 4–5 years
- **Nesting Habits:** Cavities in trees or nest boxes
- **Eggs:** 3–7 white eggs; 12–14 day incubation
- **Predators:** Snakes, raccoons, woodpeckers

DID YOU KNOW...

Prothonotary Warblers are one of only two eastern warblers that nest in cavities. Their stronghold in Maryland lies in the tidal forests of the Patuxent and Pocomoke rivers.

25- YELLOW WARBLER *(yel-oh war-blur)*

Yellow Warbler is a glowing burst of golden feathers with reddish streaks down its breast, thriving in shrubby wetlands, stream edges, and gardens across Maryland each spring and summer. Males sing sweet-sweet-sweeter-than-sweet from exposed branches, often fluttering while they call. These warblers forage for caterpillars, beetles, and spiders among new leaves and willow branches, frequently flicking their tails. Nests are compact cups built in low shrubs or saplings, and pairs may raise multiple broods. They are common across the state and are among the easiest warblers to see in migration and breeding season. Though small, they are determined defenders of their nests, often chasing away larger birds. Yellow Warblers migrate by night, wintering in Central and northern South America. Their lemony brightness adds color and song to riparian habitats from May to August.

- **Scientific Name:** Setophaga petechia
- **Habitat:** Wetlands, thickets, riversides, orchards
- **Diet:** Insects, caterpillars, spiders
- **Size / Weight:** 4.7–5.1 in / 0.3–0.4 oz
- **Lifespan:** 3–6 years average
- **Nesting Habits:** Shrubs or saplings near water
- **Eggs:** 3–6 pale eggs; 11–13 day incubation
- **Predators:** Jays, snakes, cowbirds, cats

DID YOU KNOW...

Yellow Warblers often bury cowbird eggs laid in their nests by building a new floor over them—sometimes repeating this multiple times to protect their own clutch.

Creeping up trunks like a tiny tree-climbing nuthatch, the Black-and-white Warbler wears bold zebra stripes from bill to tail. Both sexes are patterned in black and white, with males showing darker facial markings. These warblers nest in woodlands throughout Maryland and are often one of the first migrants to arrive in spring. They forage by spiraling along tree limbs and trunks, probing bark crevices for insects, spiders, and caterpillars. Their song is a high-pitched weesa-weesa-weesa repeated from mid-story perches. Nests are placed at the base of trees or stumps, often concealed by leaves or logs. They breed widely in forested parks and upland woods and depart for Central America by mid-fall. Their unusual foraging behavior and eye-catching pattern make them stand out from other warblers.

- **Scientific Name:** Mniotilta varia
- **Habitat:** Deciduous and mixed forests, parks
- **Diet:** Insects, spiders, caterpillars
- **Size / Weight:** 4.3–5.1 in / 0.3–0.4 oz
- **Lifespan:** Up to 9 years
- **Nesting Habits:** Ground nests at base of trees
- **Eggs:** 4–5 speckled white eggs; 10–12 day incubation
- **Predators:** Snakes, raccoons, skunks

DID YOU KNOW...

Black-and-white Warblers are one of the few warblers that regularly forage on tree bark, using strong legs and sharp claws to hang like a creeper.

The Cerulean Warbler is a sky-blue gem of the forest canopy, with males sporting pale underparts streaked with blue and a subtle neck band. Females are greenish-blue with creamy throats and soft facial lines. In Maryland, they're a rare breeder primarily found in mature forests like Susquehanna State Park. These birds stay high in the tallest oaks and tulip poplars, making them difficult to spot but easy to hear singing their buzzy, rising trill. Cerulean Warblers feed on insects gleaned from leaves and twigs while fluttering through the upper branches. Nests are small, cup-shaped, and tucked into horizontal limbs well above the ground. They migrate to the Andes in fall, covering thousands of miles. Due to habitat loss on both breeding and wintering grounds, this warbler is considered a species of concern.

- **Scientific Name:** Setophaga cerulea
- **Habitat:** Mature deciduous forests, high canopy
- **Diet:** Insects, caterpillars, spiders
- **Size / Weight:** 4.3 in / 0.3–0.4 oz
- **Lifespan:** Typically 3–6 years
- **Nesting Habits:** High canopy branches, 30+ ft up
- **Eggs:** 3–5 pale blue eggs; 12-day incubation
- **Predators:** Hawks, snakes, cowbirds

DID YOU KNOW...

Cerulean Warblers migrate longer distances than nearly any other eastern warbler. In Maryland, they're best seen in early May by scanning treetop canopies with binoculars.

28- CANADA WARBLER *(kan-uh-duh war-blur)*

Canada Warbler is a lively, low-foraging warbler with a bright yellow throat and breast and a necklace of black streaks across its chest. Males have bolder markings, while females are slightly duller but equally charming. Found in the cool, mossy woodlands of western Maryland's highlands, this warbler is one of the last to arrive in spring and one of the first to leave in late summer. It flits through ferns and low branches in constant motion, snapping up insects from midair or leaf surfaces. Its song is a bright, musical jumble, and nests are hidden in the moss or leaf litter at the base of shrubs or stumps. Canada Warblers breed in a narrow band of upland forest, and habitat loss has made them a conservation priority across their range. Their dark eye rings give them a "spectacled" look. Watch for them near shaded streams, tangled rhododendrons, or mountain laurel.

- **Scientific Name:** Cardellina canadensis
- **Habitat:** Cool, damp forests, stream ravines, highlands
- **Diet:** Insects, spiders, flies
- **Size / Weight:** 4.7–5.1 in / 0.3–0.5 oz
- **Lifespan:** Typically 4–5 years
- **Nesting Habits:** Ground-level nests in mossy understory
- **Eggs:** 4–5 white eggs; 12-day incubation
- **Predators:** Jays, snakes, rodents

DID YOU KNOW...

Though named "Canada," this warbler breeds in Maryland's high elevations. Its flashy yellow necklace and constant motion make it a favorite among mountain birders.

The Yellow-throated Vireo is a bright, bold forest dweller with a lemon-yellow throat, olive back, and two strong white wingbars. Unlike other vireos, its color is vibrant and unmistakable. Found in mature woodlands across Maryland in summer, especially near rivers and upland ridges, males sing a slow, burry three-eight song from high in the canopy. Pairs build hanging cup nests on forked limbs using bark, moss, and spider silk. They feed on caterpillars, flies, and beetles, gleaning insects from leaves as they move slowly through treetops. These vireos are methodical and often remain in one tree for long periods. They prefer undisturbed forest tracts and are less common in developed areas. After breeding, they migrate to Central America by mid-fall. Their song, coloration, and steady habits make them a highlight for patient forest birders.

- **Scientific Name:** Vireo flavifrons
- **Habitat:** Deciduous woods, river bluffs, mature forests
- **Diet:** Insects, caterpillars, berries
- **Size / Weight:** 5.1–5.9 in / 0.5–0.7 oz
- **Lifespan:** Up to 6 years; average 2–4
- **Nesting Habits:** Hanging cups in high horizontal branches
- **Eggs:** 3–5 white eggs; 13–15 day incubation
- **Predators:** Jays, snakes, squirrels

DID YOU KNOW...

Yellow-throated Vireos often sing the same song for hours from a single perch, making their location easier to pinpoint despite their treetop lifestyle.

The Indigo Bunting is a dazzling summer resident, with breeding males glowing electric blue from bill to tail. Females and juveniles are warm brown, often streaked. These buntings prefer brushy roadsides, woodland edges, and regenerating clearings across Maryland. Males perch on exposed twigs to deliver high, musical phrases—fire! fire! where? where?—repeating all morning long. They feed on seeds, insects, and berries, foraging in low vegetation. Nests are hidden in dense shrubs or blackberry tangles, often close to the ground. Pairs raise one to two broods before migrating at night to Central America. Indigo Buntings are drawn to open, shrubby habitats and often return to the same territories year after year. Their vibrant color and sweet song make them a summertime favorite in rural areas and open woods.

- **Scientific Name:** Passerina cyanea
- **Habitat:** Brushy fields, forest edges, roadsides
- **Diet:** Seeds, insects, berries
- **Size / Weight:** 4.5–5.9 in / 0.4–0.6 oz
- **Lifespan:** Typically 2–4 years; up to 10
- **Nesting Habits:** Shrubs or brambles, 2–5 ft above ground
- **Eggs:** 3–4 pale blue eggs; 12–13 day incubation
- **Predators:** Snakes, raccoons, jays, cats

DID YOU KNOW...

Indigo Buntings navigate by the stars during nocturnal migration. Young birds learn celestial maps by watching the night sky before their first fall flight.

RAPTORS
AND OWLS

1- BALD EAGLE *(bawld ee-guhl)*

The Bald Eagle is one of Maryland's most powerful and unmistakable raptors, with a white head and tail, dark brown body, and massive yellow bill. Adults soar on broad wings over rivers, lakes, and estuaries, often seen gliding near the Chesapeake Bay or perched in tall pines. Immature eagles are brown with mottled plumage and take five years to reach full adult coloration. They feed primarily on fish but will scavenge carrion, steal prey from other birds, or hunt waterfowl. Maryland hosts one of the East Coast's densest eagle populations, particularly at Conowingo Dam, where dozens gather each fall. Conservation efforts helped this species rebound dramatically after mid-20th century declines. Their sheer size, piercing calls, and commanding presence have made them a national icon and a majestic symbol of wild places.

- **Scientific Name:** Haliaeetus leucocephalus
- **Habitat:** Lakes, rivers, estuaries, coastal forests
- **Diet:** Fish, waterfowl, carrion
- **Size / Weight:** 27–35 in / 8–14 lbs
- **Lifespan:** 20–30 years in the wild
- **Nesting Habits:** Massive tree nests, reused yearly
- **Eggs:** 1–3 white eggs; 35-day incubation
- **Predators:** Nestlings threatened by owls or raccoons

DID YOU KNOW...

Bald Eagles congregate by the dozens at Conowingo Dam each November, drawn by easy fishing and open water—offering one of the best eagle-watching spectacles in the Eastern U.S.

Red-tailed Hawk is a sturdy, broad-winged raptor commonly seen soaring over highways, farmland, and woodlands across Maryland. Adults show rich brown backs, pale undersides, and a signature rufous-red tail, while immatures have streaked tails and darker bellies. They perch on trees, poles, and fenceposts, watching for small mammals like voles and squirrels. Red-tails hunt with sharp vision and strong talons, diving quickly when prey is spotted. Their raspy kreeeer scream is iconic, often dubbed over other birds in movies. These hawks build stick nests high in trees and may use the same site for years. Pairs are territorial and monogamous, displaying aerial courtship spirals each spring. Year-round residents in Maryland, they're also joined by northern migrants in winter. Their adaptability to open and suburban landscapes makes them one of the state's most widespread raptors.

- **Scientific Name:** Buteo jamaicensis
- **Habitat:** Forest edges, fields, suburbs, roadsides
- **Diet:** Rodents, rabbits, birds, reptiles
- **Size / Weight:** 18–26 in / 2–4.5 lbs
- **Lifespan:** Up to 25 years; average 10–15
- **Nesting Habits:** Stick nests in tall trees or cliffs
- **Eggs:** 1–3 white eggs; 28–35 day incubation
- **Predators:** Eggs vulnerable to crows, raccoons

DID YOU KNOW...

The scream used for eagles in movies is usually a Red-tailed Hawk call. Their raspy cry has become Hollywood's default raptor voice.

The Osprey is a long-winged fish hawk, easily recognized by its white head, dark eye stripe, and sharply hooked beak. It's common along Maryland's rivers and coastlines, especially the Chesapeake Bay, where it nests in abundance. Ospreys hover and plunge feet-first into water to catch fish with sharp talons and spiny footpads. They nest atop platforms, channel markers, and even cell towers, building large stick nests often reused annually. Pairs return to the same site each spring after wintering in Central and South America. Their high-pitched whistles echo over marinas, marshes, and bayside homes from March through September. Ospreys are a conservation success story—once rare due to pesticide use, they rebounded with protections and widespread nest platform efforts. Their aerial dives and fish-carrying flights make them thrilling to observe along Maryland's tidal waters.

- **Scientific Name:** Pandion haliaetus
- **Habitat:** Bays, rivers, reservoirs, coastal areas
- **Diet:** Almost entirely fish
- **Size / Weight:** 21–26 in / 2.5–4.5 lbs
- **Lifespan:** Typically 10–15 years
- **Nesting Habits:** Platforms, snags, utility poles
- **Eggs:** 2–4 speckled eggs; 35–42 day incubation
- **Predators:** Owls, raccoons, eagles

DID YOU KNOW...

Ospreys have reversible outer toes and barbed pads that help them hold slippery fish—an adaptation found in few other raptors.

Peregrine Falcon is a sleek, fast-flying raptor built for speed and precision, with long pointed wings, a barred chest, and bold facial markings. Adults are blue-gray above and finely barred below, while juveniles show more streaking. Peregrines nest on cliffs, bridges, and skyscrapers—including buildings in Baltimore—where they dive on pigeons and shorebirds from great heights. Their stoop, or hunting dive, can exceed 200 mph, making them the fastest animal on Earth. Once decimated by pesticides, they've made a dramatic comeback through nesting tower programs and urban adaptation. Peregrines return to the same site each year, forming lifelong pairs and raising their young on ledges or gravel rooftops. They're most visible near coastal cities and river crossings, especially in spring and fall migration. Their power and grace in flight make them a top prize for birdwatchers.

- **Scientific Name:** Falco peregrinus
- **Habitat:** Cliffs, cities, coastlines, bridges
- **Diet:** Birds, pigeons, shorebirds
- **Size / Weight:** 13–20 in / 1–3.5 lbs
- **Lifespan:** Up to 17 years in wild
- **Nesting Habits:** Scrapes on cliffs or tall structures
- **Eggs:** 2–5 reddish eggs; 29–32 day incubation
- **Predators:** Owls, raccoons (at nest)

DID YOU KNOW...

Peregrines once nested only on cliffs. Now they thrive in cities, where skyscrapers mimic cliffs and pigeons provide steady prey.

5- COOPER'S HAWK *(koo-pers hawk)*

Cooper's Hawk is a medium-sized, woodland raptor with short, rounded wings and a long, banded tail—perfect for weaving through trees at high speed. Adults have slate-gray backs, reddish-barred underparts, and piercing red eyes. Juveniles are brown-streaked with yellow eyes. These agile predators specialize in catching songbirds and doves in flight, often ambushing backyard feeders. Cooper's Hawks are fierce defenders of their nesting territory and raise up to five young each year. They're year-round residents in Maryland, though more visible in fall and winter when they hunt more boldly. Misidentification with Sharp-shinned Hawks is common, but Cooper's are larger with broader heads. Their stealthy movements and burst-flight style make them one of the most impressive avian hunters in the state.

- **Scientific Name:** Accipiter cooperii
- **Habitat:** Forests, parks, suburbs
- **Diet:** Songbirds, doves, squirrels
- **Size / Weight:** 14–20 in / 1–1.5 lbs
- **Lifespan:** 12 years max; avg 3–5
- **Nesting Habits:** Stick nests in tall trees
- **Eggs:** 3–5 bluish eggs; 30–36 day incubation
- **Predators:** Owls, raccoons, hawks

DID YOU KNOW...

Cooper's Hawks sometimes stun prey mid-air by crashing through vegetation—one of the few raptors to chase through tight spaces.

6- SHARP-SHINNED HAWK *(sharp-shind hawk)*

The Sharp-shinned Hawk is Maryland's smallest hawk, a nimble accipiter with short, rounded wings and a square-tipped tail. Adults are slate gray above with fine reddish barring below, while juveniles are streaked brown and cream. They specialize in catching small birds, launching surprise attacks near feeders or from woodland edges. Sharp-shinneds are secretive breeders in northern forests but are best seen in Maryland during fall migration, when they move south in large numbers. They soar with quick wingbeats and sharp turns, and often appear suddenly before vanishing into cover. Identification is tricky, as they closely resemble Cooper's Hawks—but they're smaller with thinner legs and smaller heads. Watch for them zipping low over fields or darting through trees. Their fierce hunting style and sudden ambushes reflect the agility and speed typical of forest raptors.

- **Scientific Name:** Accipiter striatus
- **Habitat:** Forests, edges, migration corridors
- **Diet:** Small birds, mice, insects
- **Size / Weight:** 9–13 in / 0.2–0.5 lbs
- **Lifespan:** Up to 12 years
- **Nesting Habits:** Dense woods, high tree nests
- **Eggs:** 3–5 bluish-white eggs; 30-day incubation
- **Predators:** Larger hawks, owls

DID YOU KNOW...

Sharp-shinned Hawks are most visible at hawk watches in fall, especially at mountain ridges where they soar south in steady, low glides.

The Broad-winged Hawk is a compact, stocky raptor with a white belly barred in cinnamon and a distinctive black-and-white banded tail. Though secretive in summer, they pass through Maryland in spectacular numbers during fall migration, forming swirling flocks called kettles. In breeding season, they favor dense eastern woodlands, where they build tree nests and feed on frogs, snakes, and rodents. Their high-pitched whistle, peeeeew, carries over forest clearings. They often hunt from low perches or while gliding slowly beneath the canopy. These hawks migrate to South America for the winter, covering thousands of miles. Most are seen in Maryland during late September, when dozens to hundreds may pass overhead in a single day. Their forest habits and dramatic group migration make them a seasonal highlight for raptor watchers.

- **Scientific Name:** Buteo platypterus
- **Habitat:** Deciduous forests, ridges, forest edges
- **Diet:** Frogs, rodents, insects, snakes
- **Size / Weight:** 13–17 in / 0.6–1.2 lbs
- **Lifespan:** Typically 4–5 years
- **Nesting Habits:** Tree nests in dense forests
- **Eggs:** 1–3 pale eggs; 28–31 day incubation
- **Predators:** Owls, raccoons, hawks

DID YOU KNOW...

Thousands of Broad-winged Hawks funnel through Maryland each fall during migration—best seen from hawk watches like Washington Monument State Park.

8- NORTHERN HARRIER *(nor-thern hair-ee-er)*

The Northern Harrier is a graceful, owl-faced hawk that skims low over marshes and meadows with long, tilted wings. Males are pale gray above with black wingtips, while females and juveniles are brown with streaked bellies. All have a white rump patch that flashes in flight. Harriers hunt by listening and watching, flying low to pounce on mice, voles, or frogs. They breed in open grasslands and wetlands, where females build nests directly on the ground. Though uncommon as breeders in Maryland, they're regularly seen in fall and winter patrolling over fields and tidal marshes. Harriers are one of the few raptors with pronounced sexual dimorphism—males and females look quite different. Their slow, buoyant flight and ground-hugging hunts make them easy to identify in the right habitat.

- **Scientific Name:** Circus hudsonius
- **Habitat:** Marshes, meadows, prairies, farmland
- **Diet:** Small mammals, birds, frogs
- **Size / Weight:** 18–20 in / 0.8–1.3 lbs
- **Lifespan:** Up to 16 years
- **Nesting Habits:** Ground nests in dense grasses
- **Eggs:** 4–6 white eggs; 29–31 day incubation
- **Predators:** Foxes, coyotes, owls

DID YOU KNOW...

Northern Harriers are the only hawks in North America with an owl-like facial disk, which helps them detect prey by sound.

9- BARRED OWL *(bard owl)*

Barred Owl is a stocky, round-headed owl with deep brown eyes and a classic hooting call: who-cooks-for-you, who-cooks-for-you-all. Its plumage is gray-brown with horizontal barring on the chest and vertical streaks below. Found in mature woodlands near water, Barred Owls hunt at night by gliding silently through trees and pouncing on mice, frogs, and small birds. They roost in cavities or dense branches during the day and become especially vocal at dusk. Pairs often call back and forth, especially in late winter and spring. They nest in tree cavities or use old hawk or squirrel nests. While mostly nocturnal, they may hunt in daylight on overcast days. Barred Owls are year-round residents in Maryland and are more often heard than seen in deep woods and river valleys.

- **Scientific Name:** Strix varia
- **Habitat:** Woodlands, swamps, riparian forests
- **Diet:** Rodents, birds, frogs
- **Size / Weight:** 16–25 in / 1.5–2.5 lbs
- **Lifespan:** Up to 20 years
- **Nesting Habits:** Cavities, large stick nests
- **Eggs:** 2–4 white eggs; 28–33 day incubation
- **Predators:** Great Horned Owls, raccoons

DID YOU KNOW...

Barred Owls lack ear tufts and have dark brown eyes—most other eastern owls have yellow eyes, making them easy to tell apart.

The Great Horned Owl is a powerful, broad-winged predator with piercing yellow eyes, bold facial disks, and feathered tufts that resemble horns. Its mottled brown plumage blends perfectly with forest shadows. Found across Maryland, it inhabits woodlands, parks, farmland, and even city edges. This owl hunts from dusk through night, preying on rabbits, rodents, skunks, birds—even other owls. Its call is a deep hoo-hoo-hoo hoo hoo, echoing through winter woods during breeding season. Nests are usually recycled stick platforms—abandoned hawk or crow nests—lined with little material. They begin nesting as early as January, with chicks hatching by March. Fiercely protective parents, Great Horneds will defend their young aggressively. Their silent flight, immense grip strength, and adaptability make them one of North America's top avian predators.

- **Scientific Name:** Bubo virginianus
- **Habitat:** Forests, suburbs, farmlands, parks
- **Diet:** Mammals, birds, reptiles, skunks
- **Size / Weight:** 18–25 in / 2–4.5 lbs
- **Lifespan:** Up to 28 years
- **Nesting Habits:** Old hawk or crow nests
- **Eggs:** 1–4 white eggs; 30–37 day incubation
- **Predators:** Rare; adults mostly apex

DID YOU KNOW...

Great Horned Owls can crush prey with 300+ pounds per square inch of grip—stronger than a human handshake.

The Eastern Screech-Owl is a small, compact owl with tufted ears and finely patterned plumage that comes in gray or reddish morphs. Perfectly camouflaged against bark, it roosts in tree cavities by day and emerges at dusk to hunt insects, mice, and small birds. Its haunting trills and descending whinnies are often heard before the owl is seen. Found throughout Maryland's woodlands, suburbs, and parks, Screech-Owls readily nest in boxes and tree holes. Pairs may raise two broods and stay in the same territory year-round. These owls are adaptable and thrive in urban areas with trees, gardens, and minimal disturbance. Despite their name, they don't actually screech; their ghostly calls add mystery to night walks and backyard evenings. Watch for them silhouetted near porch lights or back fences.

- **Scientific Name:** Megascops asio
- **Habitat:** Woodlands, suburbs, orchards, groves
- **Diet:** Insects, rodents, birds
- **Size / Weight:** 6.5–10 in / 4–8 oz
- **Lifespan:** 6–14 years
- **Nesting Habits:** Cavities or nest boxes
- **Eggs:** 2–6 white eggs; 26-day incubation
- **Predators:** Hawks, owls, raccoons

DID YOU KNOW...

Eastern Screech-Owls sometimes store live prey in nest cavities—paralyzing insects or frogs to feed chicks later.

The Barn Owl is a pale, long-winged owl with a heart-shaped face, dark eyes, and ghostly white underparts. Silent in flight and eerie in appearance, it hunts low over fields and marshes for voles, mice, and shrews. Barn Owls roost and nest in old barns, silos, church towers, and hollow trees. They're more common in Maryland's eastern counties and agricultural landscapes, especially near grasslands and marshes. Nocturnal and elusive, their blood-curdling shrieks often go unnoticed unless you're nearby at night. Pairs may raise multiple broods per year, often nesting in manmade structures. Though sensitive to cold and habitat loss, they persist where open land and quiet roosts remain. Their finely feathered faces help funnel sound to their keen ears, making them one of the most acoustically sensitive hunters in the animal kingdom.

- **Scientific Name:** Tyto alba
- **Habitat:** Grasslands, farmlands, marshes, barns
- **Diet:** Mice, voles, rats, shrews
- **Size / Weight:** 13–15 in / 1–1.5 lbs
- **Lifespan:** 4–5 years; max 15
- **Nesting Habits:** Barns, silos, hollow trees
- **Eggs:** 4–7 white eggs; 29–34 day incubation
- **Predators:** Raccoons, hawks, owls

DID YOU KNOW...

Barn Owls can locate prey in complete darkness by sound alone—catching a mouse under snow or tall grass with pinpoint accuracy.

13- SHORT-EARED OWL *(short-ehrd owl)*

The Short-eared Owl is a ground-nesting, open-country owl with mottled tan plumage, a pale face, and barely visible feather tufts. It's most often seen in Maryland during winter, gliding low over marshes and grasslands at dawn and dusk. Short-eared Owls flap slowly like moths, with buoyant, buoy-like flight and occasional hovering. They hunt small mammals, especially voles, by both sight and sound. Unlike most owls, they're frequently active during the day, especially in overcast or twilight hours. Their nesting in the state is rare and sporadic, mostly limited to large coastal wetlands. Roosts may host several individuals communally, and territorial skirmishes include wing-clapping displays. Best spotted at wildlife refuges and open preserves, these owls offer a seasonal delight for birders scanning wide, grassy fields.

- **Scientific Name:** Asio flammeus
- **Habitat:** Marshes, fields, grasslands
- **Diet:** Voles, mice, shrews
- **Size / Weight:** 13–17 in / 0.7–1.1 lbs
- **Lifespan:** 4–12 years
- **Nesting Habits:** Ground nests in grass or marsh
- **Eggs:** 4–7 white eggs; 24–29 day incubation
- **Predators:** Foxes, coyotes, owls

DID YOU KNOW...

Short-eared Owls are one of the world's most widespread owl species—found on every continent except Australia and Antarctica.

14- RED-SHOULDERED HAWK *(red-shol-derd hawk)*

The Red-shouldered Hawk is a striking, woodland raptor with rich rufous underparts, black-and-white checkered wings, and translucent crescent "windows" in flight. Its clear, whistled kee-ahhh call echoes through Maryland's moist forests and wooded swamps, especially in spring. These hawks prefer areas near water and hunt frogs, snakes, and small mammals from perch sites. They're territorial and often reuse stick nests built high in hardwood trees, returning year after year with the same mate. Unlike the open-country Red-tailed Hawk, Red-shouldered Hawks favor closed canopy forests. Their agility and keen eyesight let them snatch prey under cover, and their bold markings flash through the trees when they take flight. Once in decline, they've recovered well in many protected riparian corridors throughout the state.

- **Scientific Name:** Buteo lineatus
- **Habitat:** Wet woods, swamps, river forests
- **Diet:** Frogs, snakes, rodents
- **Size / Weight:** 17–24 in / 1–1.9 lbs
- **Lifespan:** Up to 19 years
- **Nesting Habits:** Stick nests high in forest trees
- **Eggs:** 2–4 white eggs; 30–33 day incubation
- **Predators:** Great Horned Owls, raccoons

DID YOU KNOW...

Red-shouldered Hawks often team up with crows to chase Great Horned Owls—driving predators from shared nesting areas.

The Turkey Vulture is a large, dark scavenger with broad wings, a bald red head, and a slightly dihedral flight posture. Common year-round across Maryland, it soars with slight wobbles, riding thermals over highways, fields, and forests. Despite its eerie appearance, the Turkey Vulture plays a crucial role by cleaning up carrion. Its sense of smell is highly developed—the best of any bird—allowing it to detect dead animals hidden under forest canopy. Turkey Vultures roost communally and often nest in caves, crevices, or hollow logs without adding any nesting material. They don't kill live prey, relying entirely on scavenging. When threatened, they defend themselves by vomiting foul-smelling food. Despite misconceptions, they're graceful fliers and essential to healthy ecosystems.

- **Scientific Name:** Cathartes aura
- **Habitat:** Forests, fields, roadsides, ridgelines
- **Diet:** Carrion
- **Size / Weight:** 25–32 in / 2–4 lbs
- **Lifespan:** Up to 20 years
- **Nesting Habits:** Ground, caves, hollow logs
- **Eggs:** 1–3 white eggs; 30–40 day incubation
- **Predators:** Eagles, owls, raccoons

DID YOU KNOW...

Turkey Vultures cool off by defecating on their legs and locate carcasses by smell—traits unique among raptors in North America.

WATERFOWLS
& SHOREBIRDS

Elegant and ghostly white, the Tundra Swan is a large, long-necked waterfowl that graces Maryland's coastal wetlands each winter. These migratory swans breed in the Arctic tundra and arrive in late fall, gathering in flocks that fill the air with musical, high-pitched whoo-whoo calls. Eastern Neck National Wildlife Refuge is a prime viewing site, where hundreds rest and feed in shallow bays and estuarine marshes. They forage on submerged plants by tipping forward in the water, and may also graze on grains in nearby farm fields. Their graceful flight is marked by rhythmic wingbeats and occasional trumpeting. Despite their size, they are strong long-distance migrants, flying over 3,000 miles twice a year. Their presence in Maryland is a winter spectacle and a vital part of the Chesapeake ecosystem.

- **Scientific Name:** Cygnus columbianus
- **Habitat:** Coastal marshes, estuaries, bays
- **Diet:** Aquatic plants, roots, grains
- **Size / Weight:** 45–59 in / 14–23 lbs
- **Lifespan:** Up to 20 years
- **Nesting Habits:** Breeds in Arctic, not in Maryland
- **Eggs:** 3–5 cream eggs; ~32-day incubation
- **Predators:** Eagles, foxes (eggs/young)

DID YOU KNOW...

Tundra Swans fly in family groups during migration, often calling to one another in flight—a sound that once earned them the name "whistling swan."

The Canvasback is a striking diving duck with a chestnut-red head, black breast, and sloping profile that gives it a regal look. Males are especially eye-catching with pale gray backs resembling canvas, which inspired their name. These ducks winter in large numbers across the Chesapeake Bay, where they forage in underwater beds of wild celery and other aquatic vegetation. Their broad, webbed feet and streamlined bodies make them powerful swimmers and divers. Canvasbacks often form mixed flocks with other diving ducks, especially in sheltered coves and tributaries. They are fast flyers with strong, whistling wingbeats and prefer open water over dense vegetation. The Bay is one of their most important wintering areas in North America, hosting tens of thousands annually.

- **Scientific Name:** Aythya valisineria
- **Habitat:** Bays, lakes, estuaries, tidal rivers
- **Diet:** Aquatic plants, seeds, invertebrates
- **Size / Weight:** 19–24 in / 2–3.5 lbs
- **Lifespan:** Up to 10 years
- **Nesting Habits:** Floating nests in prairie marshes
- **Eggs:** 5–11 olive eggs; ~24-day incubation
- **Predators:** Foxes, raccoons, snapping turtles

DID YOU KNOW...

Canvasbacks rely heavily on Chesapeake Bay eelgrass and wild celery—making the bay's health essential to their survival during winter months.

3- NORTHERN PINTAIL *(nor-thurn pin-tail)*

Sleek and graceful, the Northern Pintail is a medium-sized dabbling duck known for its long, pointed tail and elegant posture. Males sport chocolate-brown heads, white necks, and gray bodies, while females are mottled brown with a subtle elegance of their own. Pintails pass through Maryland during migration and are occasionally seen wintering in coastal marshes, tidal ponds, and open fields. They feed by tipping forward to reach seeds and aquatic plants, and sometimes forage in shallow floodplains and grain fields. Pintails are strong, agile fliers, often traveling in fast, darting flocks. Their soft "kew-kew" calls and slender silhouettes are distinctive features during migration. These ducks are early nesters and among the first to head north each spring.

- **Scientific Name:** Anas acuta
- **Habitat:** Wetlands, coastal marshes, flooded fields
- **Diet:** Seeds, aquatic plants, insects
- **Size / Weight:** 20–30 in / 1–2.5 lbs
- **Lifespan:** Up to 15 years
- **Nesting Habits:** Ground nests in grasslands or tundra
- **Eggs:** 6–10 olive eggs; ~23-day incubation
- **Predators:** Coyotes, gulls, raptors

DID YOU KNOW...

Nicknamed the "greyhound of the air," Northern Pintails are among the fastest ducks, reaching speeds of nearly 50 mph during flight.

4- MALLARD *(mal-urd)*

The Mallard is one of North America's most widespread and recognizable ducks. Males feature iridescent green heads, yellow bills, chestnut breasts, and gray bodies, while females are mottled brown with orange bills. Both sexes show a blue speculum edged in white on the wing. Mallards thrive in nearly every wetland habitat across Maryland—marshes, ponds, lakes, rivers, and even suburban parks. They are year-round residents, dabbling for food by tipping forward in the shallows or grazing in nearby fields. These social birds often form large mixed flocks and interbreed readily with other duck species. Their familiar quack—especially from females—is often one of the first waterfowl sounds children learn. Mallards nest on the ground near water, and their downy ducklings leave the nest within a day to follow the mother to feeding sites. They are the wild ancestor of nearly all domestic duck breeds.

- **Scientific Name:** Anas platyrhynchos
- **Habitat:** Wetlands, ponds, lakes, parks
- **Diet:** Aquatic vegetation, seeds, insects
- **Size / Weight:** 20–26 in / 2–3 lbs
- **Lifespan:** Up to 10 years
- **Nesting Habits:** Ground nests hidden in grass or brush
- **Eggs:** 8–13 pale green eggs; 23–30 day incubation
- **Predators:** Raccoons, foxes, snapping turtles

DID YOU KNOW...

Mallards are incredibly adaptable—urban pairs have been known to nest in shopping center planters, balconies, and even parking lot medians miles from natural water. Their ability to coexist with humans helps maintain strong populations across all 50 states.

The Wood Duck is one of North America's most colorful and uniquely shaped ducks, with males displaying iridescent green and purple heads, red eyes, and chestnut breasts, while females show a teardrop-shaped white eye ring and elegant gray-brown plumage. They inhabit wooded swamps, marshes, and slow-moving streams across Maryland, especially in areas with tree-lined water. Unlike most ducks, Wood Ducks nest in tree cavities or nest boxes, sometimes high above the ground. Ducklings leap bravely from the nest shortly after hatching, bouncing unharmed to the forest floor below. These dabbling ducks feed on aquatic plants, insects, and seeds, often foraging along the water's edge. Agile flyers, they can weave through dense branches with ease. Their sharp whistle and creaky call can often be heard before they're seen slipping through the reeds or flapping away low over the water.

- **Scientific Name:** Aix sponsa
- **Habitat:** Wooded swamps, ponds, slow creeks
- **Diet:** Seeds, aquatic plants, insects
- **Size / Weight:** 18–21 in / 1.5–2 lbs
- **Lifespan:** Up to 15 years
- **Nesting Habits:** Tree cavities or nest boxes
- **Eggs:** 6–15 white eggs; 28–37 day incubation
- **Predators:** Snakes, raccoons, owls

DID YOU KNOW...

Once severely reduced by habitat loss and hunting, Wood Duck numbers rebounded thanks to conservation efforts and widespread nest box programs. Today, they are one of the few native cavity-nesting ducks still thriving across their range.

The American Black Duck is a heavy-bodied dabbling duck with dark chocolate-brown plumage, a slightly lighter head, and a purplish wing patch bordered in black. It closely resembles the female Mallard but appears darker overall. Found year-round in Maryland, especially along tidal creeks, marshes, and coastal bays, black ducks are often shy and quick to flush. They feed in shallow water by dabbling or grazing, consuming plant material, seeds, and small invertebrates. This species prefers secluded wetlands and brackish estuaries, but winter flocks may gather in larger open waters. Once more abundant, populations declined due to habitat loss and hybridization with Mallards. Conservation efforts have helped stabilize numbers. Their soft, raspy quacks are more subdued than the classic Mallard call.

- **Scientific Name:** Anas rubripes
- **Habitat:** Coastal marshes, estuaries, tidal creeks
- **Diet:** Aquatic vegetation, seeds, snails
- **Size / Weight:** 20–25 in / 2–3.5 lbs
- **Lifespan:** Up to 12 years
- **Nesting Habits:** Ground nests near wetlands
- **Eggs:** 6–12 pale green eggs; 23–30 day incubation
- **Predators:** Foxes, raccoons, gulls

DID YOU KNOW...

Though shy and often overshadowed by Mallards, American Black Ducks play a critical role in Atlantic coastal ecosystems and are considered an indicator species for wetland health across the Eastern Seaboard.

The Green-winged Teal is the smallest dabbling duck in North America, easily recognized by its compact size and rapid flight. Males are dapper with a chestnut head, bold green eye patch, and a vertical white stripe on the breast. Females are mottled brown with a more subtle face pattern. Both sexes show a vivid green wing patch in flight, sometimes only visible during quick takeoff. These ducks pass through Maryland in large flocks during migration and sometimes overwinter in ice-free marshes and flooded fields. Green-winged Teals feed in shallow wetlands by dabbling and probing mud for seeds, aquatic vegetation, and insects. Agile and quick, they flush abruptly when disturbed, zigzagging low over the water. Their whistling flight calls often betray their presence in dense marsh vegetation.

- **Scientific Name:** Anas crecca
- **Habitat:** Shallow wetlands, marshes, flooded fields
- **Diet:** Seeds, aquatic plants, invertebrates
- **Size / Weight:** 12–15 in / 0.5–1 lb
- **Lifespan:** Up to 10 years
- **Nesting Habits:** Ground nests near water (not in MD)
- **Eggs:** 6–12 creamy eggs; 21–23 day incubation
- **Predators:** Raptors, snakes, foxes

DID YOU KNOW...

Despite their small size, Green-winged Teals are long-distance migrants. Some travel from Arctic breeding grounds to the Gulf Coast and even Central America, relying on stopover wetlands like those in Maryland to refuel.

8- GREAT EGRET *(grayt ee-grit)*

The Great Egret is a tall, stately wading bird with pure white plumage, a long, daggerlike yellow bill, and black legs and feet. During the breeding season, they display elegant plumes known as aigrettes that trail from their backs in flowing streams. Common in Maryland's tidal wetlands and coastal bays, these elegant hunters patiently stalk prey in shallow water—striking with a sudden jab to seize fish, frogs, or crustaceans. They are often seen standing motionless, blending into the reeds like ghostly statues before making their precise attack. Great Egrets nest in colonies high in trees, often with other wading birds like herons and ibises. Once nearly wiped out for the feather trade, they made a dramatic recovery following early conservation laws and remain a conservation success.

- **Scientific Name:** Ardea alba
- **Habitat:** Marshes, estuaries, shorelines, swamps
- **Diet:** Fish, amphibians, crustaceans
- **Size / Weight:** 35–41 in / 2–3 lbs
- **Lifespan:** Up to 15 years
- **Nesting Habits:** Tree colonies near water
- **Eggs:** 3–5 bluish eggs; 23–26 day incubation
- **Predators:** Raccoons, hawks, crows (eggs/chicks)

DID YOU KNOW...

The Great Egret became the symbol of the National Audubon Society after its feathers were in such high demand for fashion that it nearly went extinct—a cautionary tale that sparked America's early bird protection movement.

The Great Blue Heron is the largest wading bird in North America, standing over four feet tall with a long neck, shaggy plumes, and slow, powerful wingbeats. Its slate-blue body, black crown stripe, and daggerlike yellow bill make it instantly recognizable in flight or perched at water's edge. Found throughout Maryland year-round, it frequents marshes, tidal creeks, lakeshores, and even roadside ditches. Great Blue Herons feed alone, stalking prey with deliberate steps before striking with precision. Fish make up the bulk of their diet, though they'll eat frogs, snakes, and small mammals as well. Nesting occurs high in trees in colonies called heronries, often near wetlands where food is plentiful and disturbance is minimal. They are surprisingly lightweight for their size and can fly gracefully despite their large wingspan and angular profile.

- **Scientific Name:** Ardea herodias
- **Habitat:** Marshes, lakes, rivers, tidal areas
- **Diet:** Fish, amphibians, small mammals
- **Size / Weight:** 38–54 in / 4–6 lbs
- **Lifespan:** Up to 15 years
- **Nesting Habits:** Tree nests in colonies
- **Eggs:** 2–6 pale blue eggs; ~28-day incubation
- **Predators:** Eagles, raccoons, owls (eggs/chicks)

DID YOU KNOW...

Great Blue Herons are mostly solitary hunters, but they nest in large communal colonies, sometimes with dozens or even hundreds of pairs, creating a noisy and chaotic mix of croaks, bill-clattering, and graceful silhouettes.

10- TRICOLORED HERON *(try-kol-erd hair-uhn)*

Tricolored Heron is a slender, medium-sized wader with a mix of slate-blue, lavender, and white plumage, and a thin, pointed bill perfect for precision fishing. It stands out with its long neck, white belly, and rusty stripe down the fore-neck during breeding season. Though more common in the Southeast, this elegant heron is a seasonal visitor to coastal Maryland, especially on Assateague Island and nearby marshes. It actively hunts in shallow waters, darting, spinning, and pausing before striking at small fish and shrimp.

Tricolored Herons are more animated feeders than the statuesque Great Blue Heron, often appearing hyperactive as they chase prey through the shallows. Their nesting colonies are usually shared with other wading birds, and they prefer dense vegetation over open trees. They are quiet birds overall, typically uttering only a few low croaks when disturbed or defending a nest.

- **Scientific Name:** Egretta tricolor
- **Habitat:** Coastal marshes, tidal flats, lagoons
- **Diet:** Small fish, amphibians, crustaceans
- **Size / Weight:** 22–26 in / 0.7–0.9 lbs
- **Lifespan:** Up to 10 years
- **Nesting Habits:** Colonies in shrubs or mangroves
- **Eggs:** 3–5 pale blue eggs; ~24-day incubation
- **Predators:** Raccoons, crows, snakes (eggs/chicks)

DID YOU KNOW...

Despite being one of the more colorful herons in North America, the Tricolored Heron is often overlooked due to its quiet nature and its preference for secluded tidal habitats along the coast.

The Piping Plover is a small, pale shorebird with a sand-colored back, white underparts, and a distinct black collar and forehead band in breeding season. Its bright orange legs and stubby black bill add to its charm. Piping Plovers nest on Maryland's Atlantic beaches, especially Assateague Island, where they lay eggs directly on the sand amid sparse vegetation. Their soft "peep-lo" calls blend into the ocean breeze, making them easy to overlook despite their rarity. When foraging, they sprint and pause repeatedly along the tide line, picking at marine worms and crustaceans hidden beneath the sand. Due to heavy beach recreation and habitat loss, this species is listed as threatened, and nesting areas are carefully protected with signage and fencing during summer, minimizing human disturbance to delicate breeding zones.

- **Scientific Name:** Charadrius melodus
- **Habitat:** Sandy beaches, barrier islands, dunes
- **Diet:** Insects, marine worms, crustaceans
- **Size / Weight:** 6–7 in / 1.5–2 oz
- **Lifespan:** Up to 14 years
- **Nesting Habits:** Scrapes in sand above high tide
- **Eggs:** 3–4 speckled eggs; ~27-day incubation
- **Predators:** Gulls, foxes, crows

DID YOU KNOW...

Piping Plover chicks can feed themselves within hours of hatching, but rely on their parents for warmth and protection until they can fly weeks later.

American Avocet is a striking shorebird with long, powdery blue legs and a slender, upturned bill. Breeding adults sport cinnamon-colored heads and necks, contrasting sharply with black-and-white patterned wings and back. In Maryland, avocets are graceful visitors to coastal lagoons and mudflats, especially during migration. They sweep their bills side-to-side through shallow water to capture aquatic insects and crustaceans. Their elegant walk and synchronized group foraging make them mesmerizing to watch. Though most breed inland in the western U.S., increasing sightings on the Atlantic coast suggest expanding migratory stopover use. Their calls are soft, flute-like notes that carry over tidal flats. They typically feed in quiet, open wetlands and rest in small flocks.

- **Scientific Name:** Recurvirostra americana
- **Habitat:** Mudflats, tidal lagoons, salt ponds
- **Diet:** Insects, crustaceans, small aquatic invertebrates
- **Size / Weight:** 16–20 in / 10–15 oz
- **Lifespan:** Up to 15 years
- **Nesting Habits:** Ground nest near shallow water
- **Eggs:** 3–4 speckled eggs; ~23-day incubation
- **Predators:** Gulls, raccoons, foxes

DID YOU KNOW...

The American Avocet's sweeping feeding technique is called "scything"—a graceful side-to-side motion of its curved bill that filters tiny prey from the shallows.

13- BLACK SKIMMER *(blak skim-ur)*

The Black Skimmer is a highly distinctive coastal bird, instantly recognized by its striking black-and-white plumage and bizarre bill—bright orange at the base with the lower mandible much longer than the upper. This adaptation allows it to fly just above the water's surface, "skimming" for fish with its beak slicing the surface. Skimmers visit Maryland's barrier islands and sandy coastal areas in summer, often seen flying low in synchronized groups at dusk or dawn. They nest in colonies on open beaches, laying eggs in simple sand scrapes. Their barking calls and graceful, buoyant flight add a touch of drama to the shoreline. Chicks are born with equal-length bills, which grow uneven as they mature—a trait that supports their specialized feeding style.

- **Scientific Name:** Rynchops niger
- **Habitat:** Coastal beaches, sandbars, estuaries
- **Diet:** Small fish, shrimp, aquatic invertebrates
- **Size / Weight:** 15–20 in / 10–14 oz
- **Lifespan:** Up to 20 years
- **Nesting Habits:** Sand scrapes in beach colonies
- **Eggs:** 2–5 speckled eggs; ~23-day incubation
- **Predators:** Gulls, raccoons, foxes

DID YOU KNOW...

Black Skimmers are the only North American birds with lower mandibles longer than upper ones, allowing them to snatch fish in flight without fully submerging.

The Red Knot is a chunky, rob-in-sized sandpiper with a short, straight bill and remarkable stamina. In breeding plumage, it shows a rusty-red face, breast, and belly with mottled gray upperparts. Each spring, Red Knots migrate through Maryland's coastal areas, especially the lower Eastern Shore, on their 9,000-mile journey from Tierra del Fuego to the Arctic tundra. They stop to refuel on horseshoe crab eggs, which are critical for replenishing fat stores. These shorebirds feed by probing wet sand for mollusks and crustaceans, and their flocks can number in the hundreds or thousands. Due to their dependence on precise stopover conditions and sensitive food sources, Red Knots are considered a species of high conservation concern and continue to face international threats.

- **Scientific Name:** Calidris canutus rufa
- **Habitat:** Coastal beaches, tidal flats, salt marshes
- **Diet:** Mollusks, horseshoe crab eggs, marine worms
- **Size / Weight:** 9–11 in / 4.5–7 oz
- **Lifespan:** Up to 15 years
- **Nesting Habits:** Arctic ground nests (not in MD)
- **Eggs:** 3–4 greenish eggs; ~22-day incubation
- **Predators:** Gulls, jaegers, foxes (breeding grounds)

DID YOU KNOW...

Red Knots time their spring migration to match the peak spawning of horseshoe crabs—a phenomenon so precise it's studied as one of nature's greatest timing feats.

The King Rail is a large, secretive marsh bird with rich chestnut and buff plumage, barred flanks, and a slightly down-curved bill. It resembles a larger version of the Clapper Rail but favors freshwater and brackish wetlands instead of salt marshes. In Maryland, King Rails breed in dense cattail marshes and wet meadows, where they remain hidden most of the day. Their loud, grunting "kek-kek-kek" call is often the only sign of their presence. They forage by walking through vegetation and probing mud for insects, crayfish, and small fish, often staying just out of sight. Nests are built on mats of vegetation slightly above water level and are sometimes covered with a canopy of reeds for concealment. Their populations are declining due to wetland loss and water pollution, making sightings increasingly rare.

- **Scientific Name:** Rallus elegans
- **Habitat:** Freshwater/brackish marshes, wet meadows
- **Diet:** Insects, crayfish, aquatic invertebrates
- **Size / Weight:** 15–19 in / 10–16 oz
- **Lifespan:** Up to 7 years
- **Nesting Habits:** Platform nests above shallow water
- **Eggs:** 8–12 speckled eggs; ~22–24 day incubation
- **Predators:** Snakes, raccoons, large birds

DID YOU KNOW...

King Rails are so elusive that most birders locate them by sound alone—leading to the saying "you'll hear ten for every one you actually see."

BIRDWATCHING LOGBOOK

HOW TO USE
THE BIRDWATCHING LOG

Next, you'll find a dedicated log section designed to help you track and reflect on your birdwatching experiences. Whether you're out on a weekend hike, relaxing in your backyard, or exploring a new nature reserve, these pages offer a simple, organized way to document what you see.

Each log entry gives you space to capture important details about the birds you encounter—including their appearance, behavior, and location—while also helping you build lasting memories and sharpen your identification skills.

Here's a quick guide to each section of the log page:

Date, Time & Season

Record when your sighting took place. Over time, this can help you recognize seasonal patterns and migration timing.

Location, GPS, Habitat

Write down the name of the place (park, city, preserve), and note any GPS coordinates if available. Include a few words to describe the habitat (e.g., marsh, forest edge, open field).

Weather & Temperature

Weather affects bird activity. Noting the conditions—sunny, overcast, windy, etc.—adds context to your sightings.

Bird Name & Sex

Write the name of the bird you believe you've identified. If you're able to tell whether it was male or female, add that here too.

Beak Shape

Check the box that best describes the bird's beak. This can help with tricky identifications, especially for similar-looking species.

Tail Type

Select the tail shape or length that best matches what you saw. Fluffy, long, or short tails can be key field marks.

Bird's Location

Where was the bird when you saw it? Mark whether it was on the ground, perched in a tree, feeding at a feeder, etc.

Colors and Markings

Describe the bird's colors and any unique patterns—eye rings, wing bars, speckles, or chest colors, for example.

Bird Sound

Did the bird make any sounds? Check if it was singing, chirping, calling, or silent. Noting this can help identify species that are more easily heard than seen.

Number Seen

Indicate how many birds you observed. Was it a solo sighting, a pair, or a larger group? This helps track bird behavior and social patterns.

Where On the Map?

Use this space to mark or write which region, city, or preserve the sighting took place in. Over time, this will show you where your most memorable sightings occurred.

Notes

Use the notes section for anything else—maybe who you were with, what camera you used, or what made the moment special.

Rating

Use the star system to rate your sighting—whether it was rare, surprising, or just personally exciting. Make it fun and personal!

This log isn't about perfection—it's about presence. The more you record, the more you'll learn. Over time, these pages become your personal history of discovery, filled with small moments of connection that bring the world of birds to life.

Happy logging—and happy birding!

BIRD WATCHING LOG

DATE _____   TIME _____

SEASON _____   HABITAT _____

LOCATION _____   GPS _____

WEATHER _____   TEMPERATURE _____

BIRD NAME _____   SEX _____

BEAK SHAPE
- ☐ CONE
- ☐ HOOKED
- ☐ LONG-THIN
- ☐ SHORT-POINTED
- ☐ FLAT-WIDE

TAIL
- ☐ SHORT
- ☐ LONG
- ☐ WIDE
- ☐ THIN
- ☐ FLURRY

BIRD'S LOCATION
- ☐ GROUND
- ☐ TREE
- ☐ BUSH
- ☐ FEEDER
- ☐ FENCE

COLORS AND MARKINGS

BIRD SOUND ☐ CHIRP ☐ WHISTLE ☐ SONG ☐ CALL

NUMBER SEEN ☐ SOLO ☐ PAIR ☐ GROUP ☐ FLOCK

LOCATION IN MARYLAND?

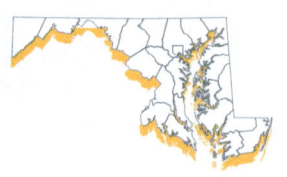

NOTES
_____
_____
_____
_____
_____
_____

BIRD RATING ☆☆☆☆☆

BIRD WATCHING LOG

DATE _____   TIME _____
SEASON _____   HABITAT _____
LOCATION _____   GPS _____
WEATHER _____   TEMPERATURE _____
BIRD NAME _____   SEX _____

BEAK SHAPE
- ☐ CONE
- ☐ HOOKED
- ☐ LONG-THIN
- ☐ SHORT-POINTED
- ☐ FLAT-WIDE

TAIL
- ☐ SHORT
- ☐ LONG
- ☐ WIDE
- ☐ THIN
- ☐ FLURRY

BIRD'S LOCATION
- ☐ GROUND
- ☐ TREE
- ☐ BUSH
- ☐ FEEDER
- ☐ FENCE

COLORS AND MARKINGS

BIRD SOUND ☐ CHIRP ☐ WHISTLE ☐ SONG ☐ CALL

NUMBER SEEN ☐ SOLO ☐ PAIR ☐ GROUP ☐ FLOCK

LOCATION IN MARYLAND?

NOTES
_____
_____
_____
_____
_____
_____

BIRD RATING ☆ ☆ ☆ ☆ ☆

BIRD WATCHING LOG

DATE _____ TIME _____

SEASON _____ HABITAT _____

LOCATION _____ GPS _____

WEATHER _____ TEMPERATURE _____

BIRD NAME _____ SEX _____

BEAK SHAPE

- ☐ CONE
- ☐ HOOKED
- ☐ LONG-THIN
- ☐ SHORT-POINTED
- ☐ FLAT-WIDE

TAIL

- ☐ SHORT
- ☐ LONG
- ☐ WIDE
- ☐ THIN
- ☐ FLURRY

BIRD'S LOCATION

- ☐ GROUND
- ☐ TREE
- ☐ BUSH
- ☐ FEEDER
- ☐ FENCE

COLORS AND MARKINGS

BIRD SOUND ☐ CHIRP ☐ WHISTLE ☐ SONG ☐ CALL

NUMBER SEEN ☐ SOLO ☐ PAIR ☐ GROUP ☐ FLOCK

LOCATION IN MARYLAND?

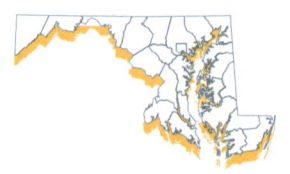

NOTES

_____
_____
_____
_____
_____
_____

BIRD RATING

BIRD WATCHING LOG

DATE _____ TIME _____

SEASON _____ HABITAT _____

LOCATION _____ GPS _____

WEATHER _____ TEMPERATURE _____

BIRD NAME _____ SEX _____

BEAK SHAPE

- ☐ CONE
- ☐ HOOKED
- ☐ LONG-THIN
- ☐ SHORT-POINTED
- ☐ FLAT-WIDE

TAIL

- ☐ SHORT
- ☐ LONG
- ☐ WIDE
- ☐ THIN
- ☐ FLURRY

BIRD'S LOCATION

- ☐ GROUND
- ☐ TREE
- ☐ BUSH
- ☐ FEEDER
- ☐ FENCE

COLORS AND MARKINGS

BIRD SOUND ☐ CHIRP ☐ WHISTLE ☐ SONG ☐ CALL

NUMBER SEEN ☐ SOLO ☐ PAIR ☐ GROUP ☐ FLOCK

LOCATION IN MARYLAND?

NOTES

_____
_____
_____
_____
_____

BIRD RATING ☆☆☆☆☆

BIRD WATCHING LOG

DATE _____   TIME _____

SEASON _____   HABITAT _____

LOCATION _____   GPS _____

WEATHER _____   TEMPERATURE _____

BIRD NAME _____   SEX _____

BEAK SHAPE
☐ CONE
☐ HOOKED
☐ LONG-THIN
☐ SHORT-POINTED
☐ FLAT-WIDE

TAIL
☐ SHORT
☐ LONG
☐ WIDE
☐ THIN
☐ FLURRY

BIRD'S LOCATION
☐ GROUND
☐ TREE
☐ BUSH
☐ FEEDER
☐ FENCE

COLORS AND MARKINGS

BIRD SOUND   ☐ CHIRP   ☐ WHISTLE   ☐ SONG   ☐ CALL

NUMBER SEEN   ☐ SOLO   ☐ PAIR   ☐ GROUP   ☐ FLOCK

LOCATION IN MARYLAND?

NOTES

_____

_____

_____

_____

_____

BIRD RATING ☆☆☆☆☆

BIRD WATCHING LOG

DATE _____   TIME _____

SEASON _____   HABITAT _____

LOCATION _____   GPS _____

WEATHER _____   TEMPERATURE _____

BIRD NAME _____   SEX _____

BEAK SHAPE
- [ ] CONE
- [ ] HOOKED
- [ ] LONG-THIN
- [ ] SHORT-POINTED
- [ ] FLAT-WIDE

TAIL
- [ ] SHORT
- [ ] LONG
- [ ] WIDE
- [ ] THIN
- [ ] FLURRY

BIRD'S LOCATION
- [ ] GROUND
- [ ] TREE
- [ ] BUSH
- [ ] FEEDER
- [ ] FENCE

COLORS AND MARKINGS

BIRD SOUND [ ] CHIRP   [ ] WHISTLE   [ ] SONG   [ ] CALL

NUMBER SEEN [ ] SOLO   [ ] PAIR   [ ] GROUP   [ ] FLOCK

LOCATION IN MARYLAND?

NOTES
_____
_____
_____
_____
_____
_____

BIRD RATING ☆☆☆☆☆

BIRD WATCHING LOG

DATE _____   TIME _____

SEASON _____   HABITAT _____

LOCATION _____   GPS _____

WEATHER _____   TEMPERATURE _____

BIRD NAME _____   SEX _____

BEAK SHAPE

- ☐ CONE
- ☐ HOOKED
- ☐ LONG-THIN
- ☐ SHORT-POINTED
- ☐ FLAT-WIDE

TAIL

- ☐ SHORT
- ☐ LONG
- ☐ WIDE
- ☐ THIN
- ☐ FLURRY

BIRD'S LOCATION

- ☐ GROUND
- ☐ TREE
- ☐ BUSH
- ☐ FEEDER
- ☐ FENCE

COLORS AND MARKINGS

BIRD SOUND ☐ CHIRP   ☐ WHISTLE   ☐ SONG   ☐ CALL

NUMBER SEEN ☐ SOLO   ☐ PAIR   ☐ GROUP   ☐ FLOCK

LOCATION IN MARYLAND?

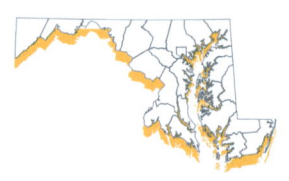

NOTES

_____

_____

_____

_____

_____

_____

BIRD RATING

BIRD WATCHING LOG

DATE _____   TIME _____

SEASON _____   HABITAT _____

LOCATION _____   GPS _____

WEATHER _____   TEMPERATURE _____

BIRD NAME _____   SEX _____

BEAK SHAPE
- ☐ CONE
- ☐ HOOKED
- ☐ LONG-THIN
- ☐ SHORT-POINTED
- ☐ FLAT-WIDE

TAIL
- ☐ SHORT
- ☐ LONG
- ☐ WIDE
- ☐ THIN
- ☐ FLURRY

BIRD'S LOCATION
- ☐ GROUND
- ☐ TREE
- ☐ BUSH
- ☐ FEEDER
- ☐ FENCE

COLORS AND MARKINGS

BIRD SOUND ☐ CHIRP ☐ WHISTLE ☐ SONG ☐ CALL

NUMBER SEEN ☐ SOLO ☐ PAIR ☐ GROUP ☐ FLOCK

LOCATION IN MARYLAND?

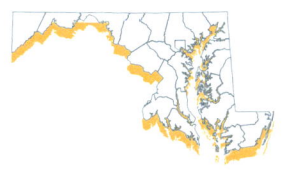

NOTES
_____
_____
_____
_____
_____
_____

BIRD RATING ☆☆☆☆☆

BIRD WATCHING LOG

DATE _____   TIME _____

SEASON _____   HABITAT _____

LOCATION _____   GPS _____

WEATHER _____   TEMPERATURE _____

BIRD NAME _____   SEX _____

BEAK SHAPE
- [ ] CONE
- [ ] HOOKED
- [ ] LONG-THIN
- [ ] SHORT-POINTED
- [ ] FLAT-WIDE

TAIL
- [ ] SHORT
- [ ] LONG
- [ ] WIDE
- [ ] THIN
- [ ] FLURRY

BIRD'S LOCATION
- [ ] GROUND
- [ ] TREE
- [ ] BUSH
- [ ] FEEDER
- [ ] FENCE

COLORS AND MARKINGS

BIRD SOUND [ ] CHIRP [ ] WHISTLE [ ] SONG [ ] CALL

NUMBER SEEN [ ] SOLO [ ] PAIR [ ] GROUP [ ] FLOCK

LOCATION IN MARYLAND?

NOTES
_____
_____
_____
_____
_____

BIRD RATING

BIRD WATCHING LOG

DATE _____   TIME _____

SEASON _____   HABITAT _____

LOCATION _____   GPS _____

WEATHER _____   TEMPERATURE _____

BIRD NAME _____   SEX _____

BEAK SHAPE	TAIL	BIRD'S LOCATION
☐ CONE	☐ SHORT	☐ GROUND
☐ HOOKED	☐ LONG	☐ TREE
☐ LONG-THIN	☐ WIDE	☐ BUSH
☐ SHORT-POINTED	☐ THIN	☐ FEEDER
☐ FLAT-WIDE	☐ FLURRY	☐ FENCE

COLORS AND MARKINGS

BIRD SOUND ☐ CHIRP ☐ WHISTLE ☐ SONG ☐ CALL

NUMBER SEEN ☐ SOLO ☐ PAIR ☐ GROUP ☐ FLOCK

LOCATION IN MARYLAND?

NOTES

_____

_____

_____

_____

_____

BIRD RATING ☆ ☆ ☆ ☆ ☆

BIRD WATCHING LOG

DATE _____ TIME _____

SEASON _____ HABITAT _____

LOCATION _____ GPS _____

WEATHER _____ TEMPERATURE _____

BIRD NAME _____ SEX _____

BEAK SHAPE
- ☐ CONE
- ☐ HOOKED
- ☐ LONG-THIN
- ☐ SHORT-POINTED
- ☐ FLAT-WIDE

TAIL
- ☐ SHORT
- ☐ LONG
- ☐ WIDE
- ☐ THIN
- ☐ FLURRY

BIRD'S LOCATION
- ☐ GROUND
- ☐ TREE
- ☐ BUSH
- ☐ FEEDER
- ☐ FENCE

COLORS AND MARKINGS

BIRD SOUND ☐ CHIRP ☐ WHISTLE ☐ SONG ☐ CALL

NUMBER SEEN ☐ SOLO ☐ PAIR ☐ GROUP ☐ FLOCK

LOCATION IN MARYLAND?

NOTES

BIRD RATING ☆☆☆☆☆

BIRD WATCHING LOG

DATE _____   TIME _____

SEASON _____   HABITAT _____

LOCATION _____   GPS _____

WEATHER _____   TEMPERATURE _____

BIRD NAME _____   SEX _____

BEAK SHAPE
☐ CONE
☐ HOOKED
☐ LONG-THIN
☐ SHORT-POINTED
☐ FLAT-WIDE

TAIL
☐ SHORT
☐ LONG
☐ WIDE
☐ THIN
☐ FLURRY

BIRD'S LOCATION
☐ GROUND
☐ TREE
☐ BUSH
☐ FEEDER
☐ FENCE

COLORS AND MARKINGS

BIRD SOUND ☐ CHIRP   ☐ WHISTLE   ☐ SONG   ☐ CALL

NUMBER SEEN ☐ SOLO   ☐ PAIR   ☐ GROUP   ☐ FLOCK

LOCATION IN MARYLAND?

NOTES
_____
_____
_____
_____
_____
_____

BIRD RATING ☆☆☆☆☆

BIRD WATCHING LOG

DATE _____ TIME _____

SEASON _____ HABITAT _____

LOCATION _____ GPS _____

WEATHER _____ TEMPERATURE _____

BIRD NAME _____ SEX _____

BEAK SHAPE
- ☐ CONE
- ☐ HOOKED
- ☐ LONG-THIN
- ☐ SHORT-POINTED
- ☐ FLAT-WIDE

TAIL
- ☐ SHORT
- ☐ LONG
- ☐ WIDE
- ☐ THIN
- ☐ FLURRY

BIRD'S LOCATION
- ☐ GROUND
- ☐ TREE
- ☐ BUSH
- ☐ FEEDER
- ☐ FENCE

COLORS AND MARKINGS

BIRD SOUND ☐ CHIRP ☐ WHISTLE ☐ SONG ☐ CALL

NUMBER SEEN ☐ SOLO ☐ PAIR ☐ GROUP ☐ FLOCK

LOCATION IN MARYLAND?

NOTES

_____

_____

_____

_____

_____

BIRD RATING ☆☆☆☆☆

BIRD WATCHING LOG

DATE _____   TIME _____
SEASON _____   HABITAT _____
LOCATION _____   GPS _____
WEATHER _____   TEMPERATURE _____
BIRD NAME _____   SEX _____

BEAK SHAPE
- ☐ CONE
- ☐ HOOKED
- ☐ LONG-THIN
- ☐ SHORT-POINTED
- ☐ FLAT-WIDE

TAIL
- ☐ SHORT
- ☐ LONG
- ☐ WIDE
- ☐ THIN
- ☐ FLURRY

BIRD'S LOCATION
- ☐ GROUND
- ☐ TREE
- ☐ BUSH
- ☐ FEEDER
- ☐ FENCE

COLORS AND MARKINGS

BIRD SOUND ☐ CHIRP ☐ WHISTLE ☐ SONG ☐ CALL

NUMBER SEEN ☐ SOLO ☐ PAIR ☐ GROUP ☐ FLOCK

LOCATION IN MARYLAND?

NOTES
_____
_____
_____
_____
_____
_____

BIRD RATING ☆☆☆☆☆

BIRD WATCHING LOG

DATE _____   TIME _____

SEASON _____   HABITAT _____

LOCATION _____   GPS _____

WEATHER _____   TEMPERATURE _____

BIRD NAME _____   SEX _____

BEAK SHAPE
- [ ] CONE
- [ ] HOOKED
- [ ] LONG-THIN
- [ ] SHORT-POINTED
- [ ] FLAT-WIDE

TAIL
- [ ] SHORT
- [ ] LONG
- [ ] WIDE
- [ ] THIN
- [ ] FLURRY

BIRD'S LOCATION
- [ ] GROUND
- [ ] TREE
- [ ] BUSH
- [ ] FEEDER
- [ ] FENCE

COLORS AND MARKINGS

BIRD SOUND   [ ] CHIRP   [ ] WHISTLE   [ ] SONG   [ ] CALL

NUMBER SEEN   [ ] SOLO   [ ] PAIR   [ ] GROUP   [ ] FLOCK

LOCATION IN MARYLAND?

NOTES
_____
_____
_____
_____
_____
_____

BIRD RATING ☆☆☆☆☆

BIRD WATCHING LOG

DATE _____   TIME _____

SEASON _____   HABITAT _____

LOCATION _____   GPS _____

WEATHER _____   TEMPERATURE _____

BIRD NAME _____   SEX _____

BEAK SHAPE
- [ ] CONE
- [ ] HOOKED
- [ ] LONG-THIN
- [ ] SHORT-POINTED
- [ ] FLAT-WIDE

TAIL
- [ ] SHORT
- [ ] LONG
- [ ] WIDE
- [ ] THIN
- [ ] FLURRY

BIRD'S LOCATION
- [ ] GROUND
- [ ] TREE
- [ ] BUSH
- [ ] FEEDER
- [ ] FENCE

COLORS AND MARKINGS

BIRD SOUND [ ] CHIRP   [ ] WHISTLE   [ ] SONG   [ ] CALL

NUMBER SEEN [ ] SOLO   [ ] PAIR   [ ] GROUP   [ ] FLOCK

LOCATION IN MARYLAND?

NOTES
_____
_____
_____
_____
_____

BIRD RATING ☆☆☆☆☆

BIRD WATCHING LOG

DATE _____   TIME _____

SEASON _____   HABITAT _____

LOCATION _____ GPS _____

WEATHER _____ TEMPERATURE _____

BIRD NAME _____ SEX _____

BEAK SHAPE	TAIL	BIRD'S LOCATION
☐ CONE	☐ SHORT	☐ GROUND
☐ HOOKED	☐ LONG	☐ TREE
☐ LONG-THIN	☐ WIDE	☐ BUSH
☐ SHORT-POINTED	☐ THIN	☐ FEEDER
☐ FLAT-WIDE	☐ FLURRY	☐ FENCE

COLORS AND MARKINGS

BIRD SOUND   ☐ CHIRP   ☐ WHISTLE   ☐ SONG   ☐ CALL

NUMBER SEEN   ☐ SOLO   ☐ PAIR   ☐ GROUP   ☐ FLOCK

LOCATION IN MARYLAND?

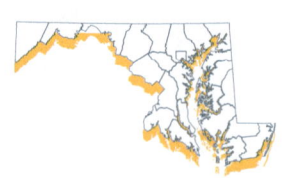

NOTES

_____
_____
_____
_____
_____
_____

BIRD RATING

BIRD WATCHING LOG

DATE _____   TIME _____

SEASON _____   HABITAT _____

LOCATION _____   GPS _____

WEATHER _____   TEMPERATURE _____

BIRD NAME _____   SEX _____

BEAK SHAPE
- ☐ CONE
- ☐ HOOKED
- ☐ LONG-THIN
- ☐ SHORT-POINTED
- ☐ FLAT-WIDE

TAIL
- ☐ SHORT
- ☐ LONG
- ☐ WIDE
- ☐ THIN
- ☐ FLURRY

BIRD'S LOCATION
- ☐ GROUND
- ☐ TREE
- ☐ BUSH
- ☐ FEEDER
- ☐ FENCE

COLORS AND MARKINGS

BIRD SOUND   ☐ CHIRP   ☐ WHISTLE   ☐ SONG   ☐ CALL

NUMBER SEEN   ☐ SOLO   ☐ PAIR   ☐ GROUP   ☐ FLOCK

LOCATION IN MARYLAND?

NOTES
_____
_____
_____
_____
_____

BIRD RATING ☆☆☆☆☆

BIRD WATCHING LOG

DATE _____   TIME _____

SEASON _____   HABITAT _____

LOCATION _____   GPS _____

WEATHER _____   TEMPERATURE _____

BIRD NAME _____   SEX _____

BEAK SHAPE
- ☐ CONE
- ☐ HOOKED
- ☐ LONG-THIN
- ☐ SHORT-POINTED
- ☐ FLAT-WIDE

TAIL
- ☐ SHORT
- ☐ LONG
- ☐ WIDE
- ☐ THIN
- ☐ FLURRY

BIRD'S LOCATION
- ☐ GROUND
- ☐ TREE
- ☐ BUSH
- ☐ FEEDER
- ☐ FENCE

COLORS AND MARKINGS

BIRD SOUND ☐ CHIRP   ☐ WHISTLE   ☐ SONG   ☐ CALL

NUMBER SEEN ☐ SOLO   ☐ PAIR   ☐ GROUP   ☐ FLOCK

LOCATION IN MARYLAND?

NOTES
_____
_____
_____
_____
_____
_____

BIRD RATING ☆ ☆ ☆ ☆ ☆

BIRD WATCHING LOG

DATE _____   TIME _____

SEASON _____   HABITAT _____

LOCATION _____   GPS _____

WEATHER _____   TEMPERATURE _____

BIRD NAME _____   SEX _____

BEAK SHAPE
- ☐ CONE
- ☐ HOOKED
- ☐ LONG-THIN
- ☐ SHORT-POINTED
- ☐ FLAT-WIDE

TAIL
- ☐ SHORT
- ☐ LONG
- ☐ WIDE
- ☐ THIN
- ☐ FLURRY

BIRD'S LOCATION
- ☐ GROUND
- ☐ TREE
- ☐ BUSH
- ☐ FEEDER
- ☐ FENCE

COLORS AND MARKINGS

BIRD SOUND ☐ CHIRP ☐ WHISTLE ☐ SONG ☐ CALL

NUMBER SEEN ☐ SOLO ☐ PAIR ☐ GROUP ☐ FLOCK

LOCATION IN MARYLAND?

NOTES
_____
_____
_____
_____
_____
_____

BIRD RATING ☆☆☆☆☆

BIRD WATCHING LOG

DATE _____   TIME _____

SEASON _____   HABITAT _____

LOCATION _____   GPS _____

WEATHER _____   TEMPERATURE _____

BIRD NAME _____   SEX _____

BEAK SHAPE
- ☐ CONE
- ☐ HOOKED
- ☐ LONG-THIN
- ☐ SHORT-POINTED
- ☐ FLAT-WIDE

TAIL
- ☐ SHORT
- ☐ LONG
- ☐ WIDE
- ☐ THIN
- ☐ FLURRY

BIRD'S LOCATION
- ☐ GROUND
- ☐ TREE
- ☐ BUSH
- ☐ FEEDER
- ☐ FENCE

COLORS AND MARKINGS

BIRD SOUND ☐ CHIRP   ☐ WHISTLE   ☐ SONG   ☐ CALL

NUMBER SEEN ☐ SOLO   ☐ PAIR   ☐ GROUP   ☐ FLOCK

LOCATION IN MARYLAND?

NOTES

BIRD RATING ☆☆☆☆☆

BIRD WATCHING LOG

DATE _____   TIME _____

SEASON _____   HABITAT _____

LOCATION _____   GPS _____

WEATHER _____   TEMPERATURE _____

BIRD NAME _____   SEX _____

BEAK SHAPE
- ☐ CONE
- ☐ HOOKED
- ☐ LONG-THIN
- ☐ SHORT-POINTED
- ☐ FLAT-WIDE

TAIL
- ☐ SHORT
- ☐ LONG
- ☐ WIDE
- ☐ THIN
- ☐ FLURRY

BIRD'S LOCATION
- ☐ GROUND
- ☐ TREE
- ☐ BUSH
- ☐ FEEDER
- ☐ FENCE

COLORS AND MARKINGS

BIRD SOUND ☐ CHIRP ☐ WHISTLE ☐ SONG ☐ CALL

NUMBER SEEN ☐ SOLO ☐ PAIR ☐ GROUP ☐ FLOCK

LOCATION IN MARYLAND?

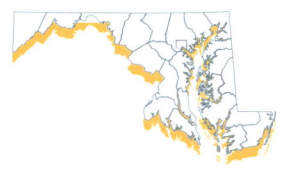

NOTES

_____
_____
_____
_____
_____

BIRD RATING

BIRD WATCHING LOG

DATE _____   TIME _____

SEASON _____   HABITAT _____

LOCATION _____   GPS _____

WEATHER _____   TEMPERATURE _____

BIRD NAME _____   SEX _____

BEAK SHAPE
- ☐ CONE
- ☐ HOOKED
- ☐ LONG-THIN
- ☐ SHORT-POINTED
- ☐ FLAT-WIDE

TAIL
- ☐ SHORT
- ☐ LONG
- ☐ WIDE
- ☐ THIN
- ☐ FLURRY

BIRD'S LOCATION
- ☐ GROUND
- ☐ TREE
- ☐ BUSH
- ☐ FEEDER
- ☐ FENCE

COLORS AND MARKINGS

BIRD SOUND ☐ CHIRP ☐ WHISTLE ☐ SONG ☐ CALL

NUMBER SEEN ☐ SOLO ☐ PAIR ☐ GROUP ☐ FLOCK

LOCATION IN MARYLAND?

NOTES
_____
_____
_____
_____
_____

BIRD RATING ☆☆☆☆☆

BIRD WATCHING LOG

DATE _____ **TIME** _____

SEASON _____ **HABITAT** _____

LOCATION _____ **GPS** _____

WEATHER _____ **TEMPERATURE** _____

BIRD NAME _____ **SEX** _____

BEAK SHAPE
- ☐ CONE
- ☐ HOOKED
- ☐ LONG-THIN
- ☐ SHORT-POINTED
- ☐ FLAT-WIDE

TAIL
- ☐ SHORT
- ☐ LONG
- ☐ WIDE
- ☐ THIN
- ☐ FLURRY

BIRD'S LOCATION
- ☐ GROUND
- ☐ TREE
- ☐ BUSH
- ☐ FEEDER
- ☐ FENCE

COLORS AND MARKINGS

BIRD SOUND ☐ CHIRP ☐ WHISTLE ☐ SONG ☐ CALL

NUMBER SEEN ☐ SOLO ☐ PAIR ☐ GROUP ☐ FLOCK

LOCATION IN MARYLAND?

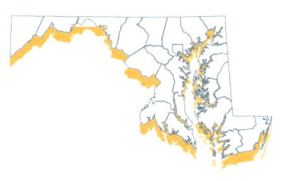

NOTES

_____
_____
_____
_____
_____
_____

BIRD RATING ☆ ☆ ☆ ☆ ☆

BIRD WATCHING LOG

DATE _____   TIME _____

SEASON _____   HABITAT _____

LOCATION _____   GPS _____

WEATHER _____   TEMPERATURE _____

BIRD NAME _____   SEX _____

BEAK SHAPE

- ☐ CONE
- ☐ HOOKED
- ☐ LONG-THIN
- ☐ SHORT-POINTED
- ☐ FLAT-WIDE

TAIL

- ☐ SHORT
- ☐ LONG
- ☐ WIDE
- ☐ THIN
- ☐ FLURRY

BIRD'S LOCATION

- ☐ GROUND
- ☐ TREE
- ☐ BUSH
- ☐ FEEDER
- ☐ FENCE

COLORS AND MARKINGS

BIRD SOUND ☐ CHIRP   ☐ WHISTLE   ☐ SONG   ☐ CALL

NUMBER SEEN ☐ SOLO   ☐ PAIR   ☐ GROUP   ☐ FLOCK

LOCATION IN MARYLAND?

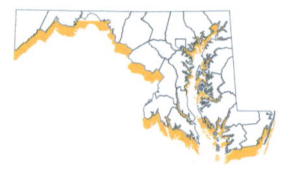

NOTES

_____

_____

_____

_____

_____

_____

BIRD RATING

BIRD WATCHING LOG

DATE _____   TIME _____
SEASON _____   HABITAT _____
LOCATION _____   GPS _____
WEATHER _____   TEMPERATURE _____
BIRD NAME _____   SEX _____

BEAK SHAPE
- [ ] CONE
- [ ] HOOKED
- [ ] LONG-THIN
- [ ] SHORT-POINTED
- [ ] FLAT-WIDE

TAIL
- [ ] SHORT
- [ ] LONG
- [ ] WIDE
- [ ] THIN
- [ ] FLURRY

BIRD'S LOCATION
- [ ] GROUND
- [ ] TREE
- [ ] BUSH
- [ ] FEEDER
- [ ] FENCE

COLORS AND MARKINGS

BIRD SOUND [ ] CHIRP [ ] WHISTLE [ ] SONG [ ] CALL

NUMBER SEEN [ ] SOLO [ ] PAIR [ ] GROUP [ ] FLOCK

LOCATION IN MARYLAND?

NOTES
_____
_____
_____
_____
_____
_____

BIRD RATING ☆☆☆☆☆

BIRD WATCHING LOG

DATE _____   TIME _____
SEASON _____   HABITAT _____
LOCATION _____   GPS _____
WEATHER _____   TEMPERATURE _____
BIRD NAME _____   SEX _____

BEAK SHAPE
- ☐ CONE
- ☐ HOOKED
- ☐ LONG-THIN
- ☐ SHORT-POINTED
- ☐ FLAT-WIDE

TAIL
- ☐ SHORT
- ☐ LONG
- ☐ WIDE
- ☐ THIN
- ☐ FLURRY

BIRD'S LOCATION
- ☐ GROUND
- ☐ TREE
- ☐ BUSH
- ☐ FEEDER
- ☐ FENCE

COLORS AND MARKINGS

BIRD SOUND ☐ CHIRP   ☐ WHISTLE   ☐ SONG   ☐ CALL

NUMBER SEEN ☐ SOLO   ☐ PAIR   ☐ GROUP   ☐ FLOCK

LOCATION IN MARYLAND?

NOTES

_____
_____
_____
_____
_____
_____

BIRD RATING ☆☆☆☆☆

BIRD WATCHING LOG

DATE _____   TIME _____
SEASON _____   HABITAT _____
LOCATION _____ GPS _____
WEATHER _____ TEMPERATURE _____
BIRD NAME _____ SEX _____

BEAK SHAPE
- [ ] CONE
- [ ] HOOKED
- [ ] LONG-THIN
- [ ] SHORT-POINTED
- [ ] FLAT-WIDE

TAIL
- [ ] SHORT
- [ ] LONG
- [ ] WIDE
- [ ] THIN
- [ ] FLURRY

BIRD'S LOCATION
- [ ] GROUND
- [ ] TREE
- [ ] BUSH
- [ ] FEEDER
- [ ] FENCE

COLORS AND MARKINGS

BIRD SOUND [ ] CHIRP [ ] WHISTLE [ ] SONG [ ] CALL

NUMBER SEEN [ ] SOLO [ ] PAIR [ ] GROUP [ ] FLOCK

LOCATION IN MARYLAND?

NOTES
_____
_____
_____
_____
_____
_____

BIRD RATING ☆☆☆☆☆

BIRD WATCHING LOG

DATE _____   TIME _____

SEASON _____   HABITAT _____

LOCATION _____   GPS _____

WEATHER _____   TEMPERATURE _____

BIRD NAME _____   SEX _____

BEAK SHAPE
- ☐ CONE
- ☐ HOOKED
- ☐ LONG-THIN
- ☐ SHORT-POINTED
- ☐ FLAT-WIDE

TAIL
- ☐ SHORT
- ☐ LONG
- ☐ WIDE
- ☐ THIN
- ☐ FLURRY

BIRD'S LOCATION
- ☐ GROUND
- ☐ TREE
- ☐ BUSH
- ☐ FEEDER
- ☐ FENCE

COLORS AND MARKINGS

BIRD SOUND   ☐ CHIRP   ☐ WHISTLE   ☐ SONG   ☐ CALL

NUMBER SEEN   ☐ SOLO   ☐ PAIR   ☐ GROUP   ☐ FLOCK

LOCATION IN MARYLAND?

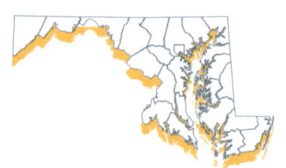

NOTES

_____
_____
_____
_____
_____
_____

BIRD RATING

BIRD WATCHING LOG

DATE _____   TIME _____
SEASON _____   HABITAT _____
LOCATION _____ GPS _____
WEATHER _____ TEMPERATURE _____
BIRD NAME _____ SEX _____

BEAK SHAPE
- ☐ CONE
- ☐ HOOKED
- ☐ LONG-THIN
- ☐ SHORT-POINTED
- ☐ FLAT-WIDE

TAIL
- ☐ SHORT
- ☐ LONG
- ☐ WIDE
- ☐ THIN
- ☐ FLURRY

BIRD'S LOCATION
- ☐ GROUND
- ☐ TREE
- ☐ BUSH
- ☐ FEEDER
- ☐ FENCE

COLORS AND MARKINGS

BIRD SOUND ☐ CHIRP ☐ WHISTLE ☐ SONG ☐ CALL

NUMBER SEEN ☐ SOLO ☐ PAIR ☐ GROUP ☐ FLOCK

LOCATION IN MARYLAND?

NOTES

BIRD RATING ☆☆☆☆☆

BIRD WATCHING LOG

DATE _____   TIME _____

SEASON _____   HABITAT _____

LOCATION _____   GPS _____

WEATHER _____   TEMPERATURE _____

BIRD NAME _____   SEX _____

BEAK SHAPE
- [ ] CONE
- [ ] HOOKED
- [ ] LONG-THIN
- [ ] SHORT-POINTED
- [ ] FLAT-WIDE

TAIL
- [ ] SHORT
- [ ] LONG
- [ ] WIDE
- [ ] THIN
- [ ] FLURRY

BIRD'S LOCATION
- [ ] GROUND
- [ ] TREE
- [ ] BUSH
- [ ] FEEDER
- [ ] FENCE

COLORS AND MARKINGS

BIRD SOUND   [ ] CHIRP   [ ] WHISTLE   [ ] SONG   [ ] CALL

NUMBER SEEN   [ ] SOLO   [ ] PAIR   [ ] GROUP   [ ] FLOCK

LOCATION IN MARYLAND?

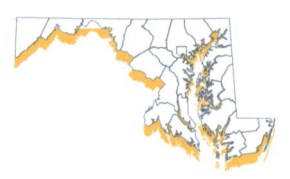

NOTES

_____
_____
_____
_____
_____
_____

BIRD RATING ☆☆☆☆☆

BIRD WATCHING LOG

DATE _____   TIME _____

SEASON _____   HABITAT _____

LOCATION _____   GPS _____

WEATHER _____   TEMPERATURE _____

BIRD NAME _____   SEX _____

BEAK SHAPE
- ☐ CONE
- ☐ HOOKED
- ☐ LONG-THIN
- ☐ SHORT-POINTED
- ☐ FLAT-WIDE

TAIL
- ☐ SHORT
- ☐ LONG
- ☐ WIDE
- ☐ THIN
- ☐ FLURRY

BIRD'S LOCATION
- ☐ GROUND
- ☐ TREE
- ☐ BUSH
- ☐ FEEDER
- ☐ FENCE

COLORS AND MARKINGS

BIRD SOUND ☐ CHIRP ☐ WHISTLE ☐ SONG ☐ CALL

NUMBER SEEN ☐ SOLO ☐ PAIR ☐ GROUP ☐ FLOCK

LOCATION IN MARYLAND?

NOTES
_____
_____
_____
_____
_____

BIRD RATING ☆☆☆☆☆

BIRD WATCHING LOG

DATE _____   TIME _____

SEASON _____   HABITAT _____

LOCATION _____   GPS _____

WEATHER _____   TEMPERATURE _____

BIRD NAME _____   SEX _____

BEAK SHAPE
- ☐ CONE
- ☐ HOOKED
- ☐ LONG-THIN
- ☐ SHORT-POINTED
- ☐ FLAT-WIDE

TAIL
- ☐ SHORT
- ☐ LONG
- ☐ WIDE
- ☐ THIN
- ☐ FLURRY

BIRD'S LOCATION
- ☐ GROUND
- ☐ TREE
- ☐ BUSH
- ☐ FEEDER
- ☐ FENCE

COLORS AND MARKINGS

BIRD SOUND ☐ CHIRP ☐ WHISTLE ☐ SONG ☐ CALL

NUMBER SEEN ☐ SOLO ☐ PAIR ☐ GROUP ☐ FLOCK

LOCATION IN MARYLAND?

NOTES
_____
_____
_____
_____
_____
_____

BIRD RATING ☆☆☆☆☆

BIRD WATCHING LOG

DATE _____   TIME _____

SEASON _____   HABITAT _____

LOCATION _____   GPS _____

WEATHER _____   TEMPERATURE _____

BIRD NAME _____   SEX _____

BEAK SHAPE
- [ ] CONE
- [ ] HOOKED
- [ ] LONG-THIN
- [ ] SHORT-POINTED
- [ ] FLAT-WIDE

TAIL
- [ ] SHORT
- [ ] LONG
- [ ] WIDE
- [ ] THIN
- [ ] FLURRY

BIRD'S LOCATION
- [ ] GROUND
- [ ] TREE
- [ ] BUSH
- [ ] FEEDER
- [ ] FENCE

COLORS AND MARKINGS

BIRD SOUND [ ] CHIRP [ ] WHISTLE [ ] SONG [ ] CALL

NUMBER SEEN [ ] SOLO [ ] PAIR [ ] GROUP [ ] FLOCK

LOCATION IN MARYLAND?

NOTES
_____
_____
_____
_____
_____

BIRD RATING ☆ ☆ ☆ ☆ ☆

BIRD WATCHING LOG

DATE _____ TIME _____

SEASON _____ HABITAT _____

LOCATION _____ GPS _____

WEATHER _____ TEMPERATURE _____

BIRD NAME _____ SEX _____

BEAK SHAPE
- ☐ CONE
- ☐ HOOKED
- ☐ LONG-THIN
- ☐ SHORT-POINTED
- ☐ FLAT-WIDE

TAIL
- ☐ SHORT
- ☐ LONG
- ☐ WIDE
- ☐ THIN
- ☐ FLURRY

BIRD'S LOCATION
- ☐ GROUND
- ☐ TREE
- ☐ BUSH
- ☐ FEEDER
- ☐ FENCE

COLORS AND MARKINGS

BIRD SOUND ☐ CHIRP ☐ WHISTLE ☐ SONG ☐ CALL

NUMBER SEEN ☐ SOLO ☐ PAIR ☐ GROUP ☐ FLOCK

LOCATION IN MARYLAND?

NOTES
_____
_____
_____
_____
_____

BIRD RATING ☆☆☆☆☆

BIRD WATCHING LOG

DATE _____   TIME _____

SEASON _____   HABITAT _____

LOCATION _____   GPS _____

WEATHER _____   TEMPERATURE _____

BIRD NAME _____   SEX _____

BEAK SHAPE
- [ ] CONE
- [ ] HOOKED
- [ ] LONG-THIN
- [ ] SHORT-POINTED
- [ ] FLAT-WIDE

TAIL
- [ ] SHORT
- [ ] LONG
- [ ] WIDE
- [ ] THIN
- [ ] FLURRY

BIRD'S LOCATION
- [ ] GROUND
- [ ] TREE
- [ ] BUSH
- [ ] FEEDER
- [ ] FENCE

COLORS AND MARKINGS

BIRD SOUND [ ] CHIRP   [ ] WHISTLE   [ ] SONG   [ ] CALL

NUMBER SEEN [ ] SOLO   [ ] PAIR   [ ] GROUP   [ ] FLOCK

LOCATION IN MARYLAND?

NOTES

_____

_____

_____

_____

_____

BIRD RATING ☆ ☆ ☆ ☆ ☆

BIRD WATCHING LOG

DATE _____   TIME _____
SEASON _____   HABITAT _____
LOCATION _____   GPS _____
WEATHER _____   TEMPERATURE _____
BIRD NAME _____   SEX _____

BEAK SHAPE
- ☐ CONE
- ☐ HOOKED
- ☐ LONG-THIN
- ☐ SHORT-POINTED
- ☐ FLAT-WIDE

TAIL
- ☐ SHORT
- ☐ LONG
- ☐ WIDE
- ☐ THIN
- ☐ FLURRY

BIRD'S LOCATION
- ☐ GROUND
- ☐ TREE
- ☐ BUSH
- ☐ FEEDER
- ☐ FENCE

COLORS AND MARKINGS

BIRD SOUND   ☐ CHIRP   ☐ WHISTLE   ☐ SONG   ☐ CALL

NUMBER SEEN   ☐ SOLO   ☐ PAIR   ☐ GROUP   ☐ FLOCK

LOCATION IN MARYLAND?

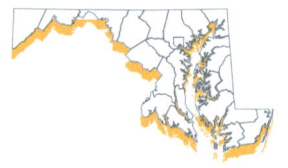

NOTES

_____
_____
_____
_____
_____
_____

BIRD RATING

BIRD WATCHING LOG

DATE _____   TIME _____

SEASON _____   HABITAT _____

LOCATION _____   GPS _____

WEATHER _____   TEMPERATURE _____

BIRD NAME _____   SEX _____

BEAK SHAPE
- ☐ CONE
- ☐ HOOKED
- ☐ LONG-THIN
- ☐ SHORT-POINTED
- ☐ FLAT-WIDE

TAIL
- ☐ SHORT
- ☐ LONG
- ☐ WIDE
- ☐ THIN
- ☐ FLURRY

BIRD'S LOCATION
- ☐ GROUND
- ☐ TREE
- ☐ BUSH
- ☐ FEEDER
- ☐ FENCE

COLORS AND MARKINGS

BIRD SOUND   ☐ CHIRP   ☐ WHISTLE   ☐ SONG   ☐ CALL

NUMBER SEEN   ☐ SOLO   ☐ PAIR   ☐ GROUP   ☐ FLOCK

LOCATION IN MARYLAND?

NOTES
_____
_____
_____
_____
_____
_____

BIRD RATING ☆☆☆☆☆

BIRD WATCHING LOG

DATE _____   TIME _____

SEASON _____   HABITAT _____

LOCATION _____   GPS _____

WEATHER _____   TEMPERATURE _____

BIRD NAME _____   SEX _____

BEAK SHAPE
- ☐ CONE
- ☐ HOOKED
- ☐ LONG-THIN
- ☐ SHORT-POINTED
- ☐ FLAT-WIDE

TAIL
- ☐ SHORT
- ☐ LONG
- ☐ WIDE
- ☐ THIN
- ☐ FLURRY

BIRD'S LOCATION
- ☐ GROUND
- ☐ TREE
- ☐ BUSH
- ☐ FEEDER
- ☐ FENCE

COLORS AND MARKINGS

BIRD SOUND   ☐ CHIRP   ☐ WHISTLE   ☐ SONG   ☐ CALL

NUMBER SEEN   ☐ SOLO   ☐ PAIR   ☐ GROUP   ☐ FLOCK

LOCATION IN MARYLAND?

NOTES
_____
_____
_____
_____
_____

BIRD RATING

BIRD WATCHING LOG

DATE _____   TIME _____

SEASON _____   HABITAT _____

LOCATION _____   GPS _____

WEATHER _____   TEMPERATURE _____

BIRD NAME _____   SEX _____

BEAK SHAPE
- ☐ CONE
- ☐ HOOKED
- ☐ LONG-THIN
- ☐ SHORT-POINTED
- ☐ FLAT-WIDE

TAIL
- ☐ SHORT
- ☐ LONG
- ☐ WIDE
- ☐ THIN
- ☐ FLURRY

BIRD'S LOCATION
- ☐ GROUND
- ☐ TREE
- ☐ BUSH
- ☐ FEEDER
- ☐ FENCE

COLORS AND MARKINGS

BIRD SOUND   ☐ CHIRP   ☐ WHISTLE   ☐ SONG   ☐ CALL

NUMBER SEEN   ☐ SOLO   ☐ PAIR   ☐ GROUP   ☐ FLOCK

LOCATION IN MARYLAND?

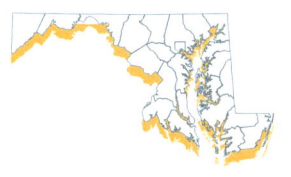

NOTES
_____
_____
_____
_____
_____
_____

BIRD RATING ☆ ☆ ☆ ☆ ☆

BIRD WATCHING LOG

DATE _____   TIME _____

SEASON _____   HABITAT _____

LOCATION _____   GPS _____

WEATHER _____   TEMPERATURE _____

BIRD NAME _____   SEX _____

BEAK SHAPE
- ☐ CONE
- ☐ HOOKED
- ☐ LONG-THIN
- ☐ SHORT-POINTED
- ☐ FLAT-WIDE

TAIL
- ☐ SHORT
- ☐ LONG
- ☐ WIDE
- ☐ THIN
- ☐ FLURRY

BIRD'S LOCATION
- ☐ GROUND
- ☐ TREE
- ☐ BUSH
- ☐ FEEDER
- ☐ FENCE

COLORS AND MARKINGS

BIRD SOUND ☐ CHIRP ☐ WHISTLE ☐ SONG ☐ CALL

NUMBER SEEN ☐ SOLO ☐ PAIR ☐ GROUP ☐ FLOCK

LOCATION IN MARYLAND?

NOTES
_____
_____
_____
_____
_____

BIRD RATING ☆☆☆☆☆

BIRD WATCHING LOG

DATE _____ TIME _____

SEASON _____ HABITAT _____

LOCATION _____ GPS _____

WEATHER _____ TEMPERATURE _____

BIRD NAME _____ SEX _____

BEAK SHAPE
- ☐ CONE
- ☐ HOOKED
- ☐ LONG-THIN
- ☐ SHORT-POINTED
- ☐ FLAT-WIDE

TAIL
- ☐ SHORT
- ☐ LONG
- ☐ WIDE
- ☐ THIN
- ☐ FLURRY

BIRD'S LOCATION
- ☐ GROUND
- ☐ TREE
- ☐ BUSH
- ☐ FEEDER
- ☐ FENCE

COLORS AND MARKINGS

BIRD SOUND ☐ CHIRP ☐ WHISTLE ☐ SONG ☐ CALL

NUMBER SEEN ☐ SOLO ☐ PAIR ☐ GROUP ☐ FLOCK

LOCATION IN MARYLAND?

NOTES
_____
_____
_____
_____
_____

BIRD RATING ☆☆☆☆☆

BIRD WATCHING LOG

DATE _____   TIME _____
SEASON _____   HABITAT _____
LOCATION _____   GPS _____
WEATHER _____   TEMPERATURE _____
BIRD NAME _____   SEX _____

BEAK SHAPE
- ☐ CONE
- ☐ HOOKED
- ☐ LONG-THIN
- ☐ SHORT-POINTED
- ☐ FLAT-WIDE

TAIL
- ☐ SHORT
- ☐ LONG
- ☐ WIDE
- ☐ THIN
- ☐ FLURRY

BIRD'S LOCATION
- ☐ GROUND
- ☐ TREE
- ☐ BUSH
- ☐ FEEDER
- ☐ FENCE

COLORS AND MARKINGS

BIRD SOUND   ☐ CHIRP   ☐ WHISTLE   ☐ SONG   ☐ CALL

NUMBER SEEN   ☐ SOLO   ☐ PAIR   ☐ GROUP   ☐ FLOCK

LOCATION IN MARYLAND?

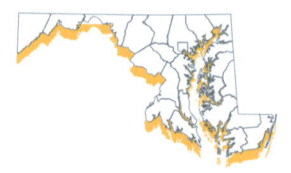

NOTES

_____
_____
_____
_____
_____

BIRD RATING

BIRD WATCHING LOG

DATE _____   TIME _____
SEASON _____   HABITAT _____
LOCATION _____   GPS _____
WEATHER _____   TEMPERATURE _____
BIRD NAME _____   SEX _____

BEAK SHAPE
- [ ] CONE
- [ ] HOOKED
- [ ] LONG-THIN
- [ ] SHORT-POINTED
- [ ] FLAT-WIDE

TAIL
- [ ] SHORT
- [ ] LONG
- [ ] WIDE
- [ ] THIN
- [ ] FLURRY

BIRD'S LOCATION
- [ ] GROUND
- [ ] TREE
- [ ] BUSH
- [ ] FEEDER
- [ ] FENCE

COLORS AND MARKINGS

BIRD SOUND   [ ] CHIRP   [ ] WHISTLE   [ ] SONG   [ ] CALL

NUMBER SEEN   [ ] SOLO   [ ] PAIR   [ ] GROUP   [ ] FLOCK

LOCATION IN MARYLAND?

NOTES

_____
_____
_____
_____
_____

BIRD RATING

BIRD WATCHING LOG

DATE _____ TIME _____

SEASON _____ HABITAT _____

LOCATION _____ GPS _____

WEATHER _____ TEMPERATURE _____

BIRD NAME _____ SEX _____

BEAK SHAPE
- ☐ CONE
- ☐ HOOKED
- ☐ LONG-THIN
- ☐ SHORT-POINTED
- ☐ FLAT-WIDE

TAIL
- ☐ SHORT
- ☐ LONG
- ☐ WIDE
- ☐ THIN
- ☐ FLURRY

BIRD'S LOCATION
- ☐ GROUND
- ☐ TREE
- ☐ BUSH
- ☐ FEEDER
- ☐ FENCE

COLORS AND MARKINGS

BIRD SOUND   ☐ CHIRP   ☐ WHISTLE   ☐ SONG   ☐ CALL

NUMBER SEEN   ☐ SOLO   ☐ PAIR   ☐ GROUP   ☐ FLOCK

LOCATION IN MARYLAND?

NOTES

_____
_____
_____
_____
_____

BIRD RATING ☆☆☆☆☆

BIRD WATCHING LOG

DATE _____   TIME _____

SEASON _____   HABITAT _____

LOCATION _____   GPS _____

WEATHER _____   TEMPERATURE _____

BIRD NAME _____   SEX _____

BEAK SHAPE
- [ ] CONE
- [ ] HOOKED
- [ ] LONG-THIN
- [ ] SHORT-POINTED
- [ ] FLAT-WIDE

TAIL
- [ ] SHORT
- [ ] LONG
- [ ] WIDE
- [ ] THIN
- [ ] FLURRY

BIRD'S LOCATION
- [ ] GROUND
- [ ] TREE
- [ ] BUSH
- [ ] FEEDER
- [ ] FENCE

COLORS AND MARKINGS

BIRD SOUND [ ] CHIRP   [ ] WHISTLE   [ ] SONG   [ ] CALL

NUMBER SEEN [ ] SOLO   [ ] PAIR   [ ] GROUP   [ ] FLOCK

LOCATION IN MARYLAND?

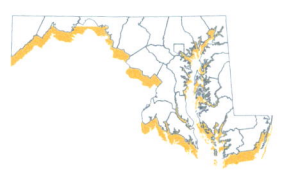

NOTES

_____
_____
_____
_____
_____

BIRD RATING ☆☆☆☆☆

BIRD WATCHING LOG

DATE _____   TIME _____

SEASON _____   HABITAT _____

LOCATION _____   GPS _____

WEATHER _____   TEMPERATURE _____

BIRD NAME _____   SEX _____

BEAK SHAPE
- [ ] CONE
- [ ] HOOKED
- [ ] LONG-THIN
- [ ] SHORT-POINTED
- [ ] FLAT-WIDE

TAIL
- [ ] SHORT
- [ ] LONG
- [ ] WIDE
- [ ] THIN
- [ ] FLURRY

BIRD'S LOCATION
- [ ] GROUND
- [ ] TREE
- [ ] BUSH
- [ ] FEEDER
- [ ] FENCE

COLORS AND MARKINGS

BIRD SOUND [ ] CHIRP [ ] WHISTLE [ ] SONG [ ] CALL

NUMBER SEEN [ ] SOLO [ ] PAIR [ ] GROUP [ ] FLOCK

LOCATION IN MARYLAND?

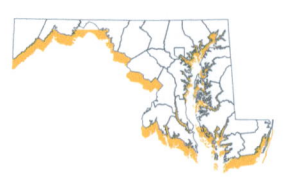

NOTES
_____
_____
_____
_____
_____

BIRD RATING

BIRD WATCHING LOG

DATE _____   TIME _____

SEASON _____   HABITAT _____

LOCATION _____   GPS _____

WEATHER _____   TEMPERATURE _____

BIRD NAME _____   SEX _____

BEAK SHAPE
- [ ] CONE
- [ ] HOOKED
- [ ] LONG-THIN
- [ ] SHORT-POINTED
- [ ] FLAT-WIDE

TAIL
- [ ] SHORT
- [ ] LONG
- [ ] WIDE
- [ ] THIN
- [ ] FLURRY

BIRD'S LOCATION
- [ ] GROUND
- [ ] TREE
- [ ] BUSH
- [ ] FEEDER
- [ ] FENCE

COLORS AND MARKINGS

BIRD SOUND   [ ] CHIRP   [ ] WHISTLE   [ ] SONG   [ ] CALL

NUMBER SEEN   [ ] SOLO   [ ] PAIR   [ ] GROUP   [ ] FLOCK

LOCATION IN MARYLAND?

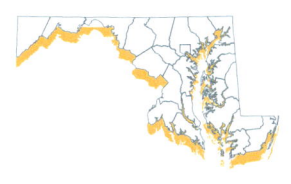

NOTES

_____
_____
_____
_____
_____
_____

BIRD RATING ☆ ☆ ☆ ☆ ☆

BIRD WATCHING LOG

DATE _____   TIME _____

SEASON _____   HABITAT _____

LOCATION _____   GPS _____

WEATHER _____   TEMPERATURE _____

BIRD NAME _____   SEX _____

BEAK SHAPE
- [ ] CONE
- [ ] HOOKED
- [ ] LONG-THIN
- [ ] SHORT-POINTED
- [ ] FLAT-WIDE

TAIL
- [ ] SHORT
- [ ] LONG
- [ ] WIDE
- [ ] THIN
- [ ] FLURRY

BIRD'S LOCATION
- [ ] GROUND
- [ ] TREE
- [ ] BUSH
- [ ] FEEDER
- [ ] FENCE

COLORS AND MARKINGS

BIRD SOUND [ ] CHIRP [ ] WHISTLE [ ] SONG [ ] CALL

NUMBER SEEN [ ] SOLO [ ] PAIR [ ] GROUP [ ] FLOCK

LOCATION IN MARYLAND?

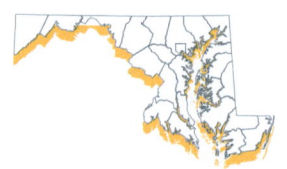

NOTES

_____
_____
_____
_____
_____
_____

BIRD RATING

CONSERVATION IN MARYLAND

Maryland's remarkable bird diversity is supported by its blend of tidal marshes, deciduous forests, rolling farmland, and Appalachian highlands—but these precious habitats are increasingly under stress. Urban expansion, sea-level rise, agricultural runoff, and climate change are all reshaping the landscapes that birds depend on to nest, feed, and migrate.

Iconic species like the Saltmarsh Sparrow, King Rail, and Cerulean Warbler are especially vulnerable to these changes. Coastal marshes are drowning under higher tides. Forest corridors are fragmented by roads and housing. And warming winters are disrupting traditional migration and breeding patterns. The challenges are real—but so are the efforts to respond.

Maryland benefits from a strong network of conservation organizations working to protect birds and their habitats. Groups like the Maryland Ornithological Society, Chesapeake Bay Foundation, and the Maryland Department of Natural Resources coordinate research, advocacy, and restoration. From creating living shorelines to replanting native forests, their efforts are making a measurable impact.

As a birder, your participation matters. Every respectful observation, every shared checklist, every backyard improvement contributes to a culture of stewardship. You can make a difference by:

- Reporting bird sightings to eBird and other citizen science platforms
- Volunteering with local wildlife centers or conservation groups
- Planting native shrubs and trees that support insects and nesting birds

- Keeping cats indoors and dogs leashed near nesting sites
- Speaking up for open space, clean water, and funding for nature

Birding is more than a pastime—it's a relationship. Every time you step outside and tune in to birdsong, you're reconnecting with a wild, shared world. And in doing so, you help protect it for the future.

In Maryland, the waters are tidal, the birds are many, and the opportunity to protect what's beautiful is always close at hand.

Many of Maryland's most vital bird habitats lie on working lands—family farms, private forests, and restored wetlands that serve as essential migration stopovers. Forward-thinking conservation easements and incentive programs are helping landowners preserve these spaces while maintaining their livelihoods. When conservation and community work hand in hand, both birds and people benefit.

Education also plays a crucial role in Maryland's conservation future. From Audubon chapters and schoolyard habitat programs to events like the Delmarva Birding Weekend and Youth Birding Days, opportunities abound for families and young people to connect with birds. By sparking curiosity and a sense of belonging in nature, these programs ensure that the birds of Maryland—and the habitats they call home—will be cherished for generations to come.

THE JOURNEY CONTINUES

As you reach the final pages of this guide, know that your birdwatching journey is far from over—in fact, it may be just beginning. Each bird you've read about in these pages is an invitation to step outside, listen more closely, and see the world with a renewed sense of wonder.

Birdwatching is a practice in patience, curiosity, and appreciation. It teaches us to slow down, to notice the quiet details, and to find joy in the flutter of wings or the distant call of a songbird. The more time you spend with birds, the more you begin to realize: they're not just passing wildlife—they're neighbors, storytellers, and reminders of the natural rhythm that still surrounds us.

Whether you're watching a cardinal at your backyard feeder or hiking through a remote preserve in search of a rare migrant, every sighting has meaning. With each new encounter, you add to your knowledge, your awareness, and your connection to the world around you.

This book was created not just to help you identify birds—but to help you fall in love with them. To encourage you to keep learning, keep exploring, and keep protecting the wild places that birds call home. Because when we protect their habitats, we also preserve something essential for ourselves: peace, beauty, and balance.

So go forward with binoculars in hand and an open heart. There are still birds waiting to be seen, trails waiting to be walked, and quiet moments waiting to be remembered.

The journey continues—one bird at a time.

We'd Love
Your Feedback!

Thank you for joining us on this birdwatching journey!

If you enjoyed this book or found it helpful during your outdoor adventures, we'd truly appreciate it if you could take a moment to leave a review on Amazon.

Your feedback not only helps us grow, but also helps fellow bird lovers discover this guide and enjoy it just as much as you did.

Made in the USA
Columbia, SC
12 July 2025

60676263R00078